Collins
revision guides

Do**Brilliantly**

KS3 Maths

The **best** approach to test preparation

- **Kevin Evans**
- **Keith Gordon**
- **Series Editor: Jayne de Courcy**

Published by HarperCollins*Publishers* Ltd
77–85 Fulham Palace Road
London W6 8JB

www.**Collins**Education.com
On-line support for schools and colleges

First published 2001. Reprinted 2001, 2002
This new cover edition published 2003

ISBN 0 00 715913 7

British Library Cataloguing in Publication Data
A catalogue record for this book is available from the British Library

Edited by Joan Miller
Production by Jack Murphy
Design by Gecko Limited
Printed and bound in China by Imago

Acknowledgements
The Author and Publishers are grateful to the following for permission to
reproduce copyright material:
1998 Key Stage 3 Mathematics Test Questions, QCA (1997)

Illustrations
Qualifications and Curriculum Authority
Gecko Ltd

Every effort has been made to contact the holders of copyright material, but if any
have been inadvertently overlooked, the Publishers will be pleased to make the
necessary arrangements at the first opportunity.

You might also like to visit:
www.**fire**and**water**.co.uk
The book lover's website

Contents

About the Maths National Test

When is the Test?

You will sit your Maths National Test in May of Year 9. Your teacher will give you the exact dates.

What does the Test cover?

The Maths curriculum is divided into four Attainment Targets. The Test covers three of these:

Ma2 Number and Algebra
Ma3 Shape, Space and Measures
Ma4 Handling Data

Your teacher assesses Ma1, 'Using and Applying Mathematics', through your coursework.

How many papers are there?

You take two Test papers – Paper 1 and Paper 2 – and a Mental arithmetic test.

The Test papers are set at four different tiers:

The tiers overlap and some of the questions are the same across the overlapping tiers.

If you take the Tier 3–5 paper, you can achieve a level 3, 4 or 5. If you take the Tier 4–6 paper, you can achieve a level 4, 5 or 6, and so on. Everyone has to take a Test in one of these tiers. Your teacher will decide which tier will best allow you to show what you know and understand about Maths.

LEVEL	LEVEL	LEVEL
3	4	5

LEVEL	LEVEL	LEVEL
4	5	6

LEVEL	LEVEL	LEVEL
5	6	7

LEVEL	LEVEL	LEVEL
6	7	8

Can I use a calculator?

You can only use a calculator in Paper 2.

What is a good grade?

By the end of Key Stage 3, most pupils are between levels 3 and 7. A typical 14 year old will achieve a level 5 or 6 in their National Test.

Exceptional performance	●	considerably better than the expected level
Level 8	●	
Level 7	●	better than the expected level
Level 6	●	expected level for 14 year olds
Level 5	●	
Level 4	●	
Level 3	●	working towards the expected level
Level 2	●	
Level 1	●	
Age	**14 years**	

How this book can help boost your Test result

1 Practise the right tier
– no Test surprises

This book contains a complete Paper 1 and a complete Paper 2 **at all four tiers**. It is clearly marked where each tier begins and ends.

Your teacher will tell you which tier you will be entered for. You can then work through the complete Paper 1 and Paper 2 for that tier.

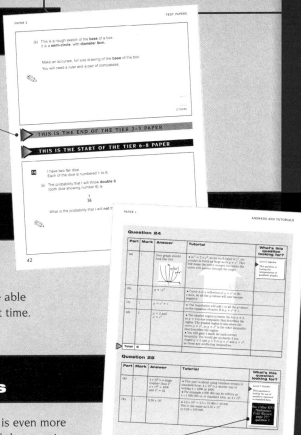

2 Answers and Tutorials
– to boost your grade

Detailed tutorial guidance is given in addition to the correct answer for each question.

This means that if you get an answer wrong, you will be able to see where you went wrong and learn what to do next time.

3 'What the examiner wants'
– inside help from the experts

In the 'What's this question looking for?' section, there is even more help. This tells you exactly which maths concept or skill the question was written to test. It also tells you which chapter of **Collins KS3 Maths Total Revision** will help you with the topic.

4 Practise for the Mental arithmetic test

This book contains three Mental arithmetic tests. This is how the Mental tests need to be set:

- Find a friend or parent to read you the questions. (In the National Test the questions will be on a tape which your teacher will play to you.)
- Select the answer sheet from the back of this book. You will need to cut out the sheet or photocopy it.

- Work out all the answers in your head and write them in the boxes on the answer sheet.
- Each question will be read to you twice and you will be given a set amount of time to answer each question.

5 Practise working under Test conditions

- Choose somewhere quiet to work while you are doing the Test.
- Make sure you have everything you need: pen, pencil, rubber, ruler, protractor and calculator.
- In the Test you will be allowed 1 hour to complete each paper. To get used to working under timed conditions, don't spend more than 1 hour on each paper.

- Leave time to check your answers carefully within the 1 hour.
- Do Paper 1 and Paper 2 on separate days. You won't sit both papers on the same day when it comes to your actual Test.

If you use this book properly, it will give you the best possible preparation for your actual Test – and help you achieve your best Test score.

How to calculate your level

To find out what level you have achieved, add up the marks you got on the Mental arithmetic test and Papers 1 and 2. Remember: you must do Mental arithmetic test C if you do the Tier 3–5 papers.

The table below shows you the marks for each level at each tier. (N means no level awarded.)

Level	Tier 3–5	Tier 4–6	Tier 5–7	Tier 6–8
N	0–25	0–25	0–30	0–38
2	26–31			
3	32–71	26–31		
4	72–106	32–62	31–36	
5	107+	63–91	37–61	39–44
6		92+	62–98	45–71
7			99+	72–108
8				109+

You might want to try papers at more than one tier. For example, if you did the Tier 3–5 papers and Mental arithmetic test C and scored more than 107 altogether, this means that you have achieved a level 5. You could then try the Tier 4–6 papers (and Mental arithmetic test A or B) to see if you can get a total of more than 92. If so, you would achieve a level 6. Your teacher will give you advice about which tier to enter in the actual Test.

Formulae

You might need to use these formulae.

AREA

Circle

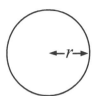

πr^2

Take π as 3.14 or use the π button on your calculator.

Triangle

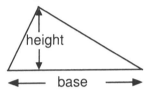

$$\frac{\text{base} \times \text{height}}{2}$$

Parallelogram

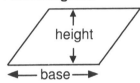

base × height

Trapezium

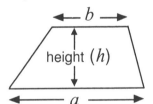

$$\frac{(a + b) \times h}{2}$$

LENGTH

Circle

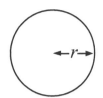

circumference = $2\pi r$

For a right-angled triangle

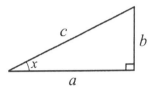

$a^2 + b^2 = c^2$ (Pythagoras' theorem)

$a = c \cos x \qquad \cos x = \dfrac{a}{c}$

$b = c \sin x \qquad \sin x = \dfrac{b}{c}$

$b = a \tan x \qquad \tan x = \dfrac{b}{a}$

VOLUME

Prism

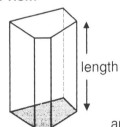

area of cross-section × length

Instructions

Answers

This means: show your working and write down your answer.

Calculators

You **must not** use a calculator to answer any question in this test.

Calculators

You **may** use a calculator to answer any question in this test if you want to.

1

Paper 1

THIS IS THE START OF THE TIER 3–5 PAPER

1   Look at this bus timetable, from Highbury to Colton:

Calculators

You **must not** use a calculator to answer any question in this test.

Bus Timetable Highbury to Colton					
Highbury *depart:*	07:45	08:30	09:30	10:45	11:30
Colton *arrive:*	08:30	09:15	10:15	11:30	12:15

(a)   A bus leaves **Highbury** at **08:30**
      What time does it arrive in **Colton?**   9.15

....
1 mark

How much time does the bus journey take?

. . . . 45 . . . . . minutes

....
1 mark

(b)   5 friends are going from Highbury to Colton by bus.
      They want to **arrive by 10:30**
      Which is the **latest** bus they can catch from Highbury?   9.30

....
1 mark

(c)   Each bus ticket costs **£2.20**
      How much do the **5** bus tickets cost altogether?

£   11.00

....
1 mark

2   (a)   **Two** of these angles are the **same size**.
              Put rings around the two angles which are the same size.

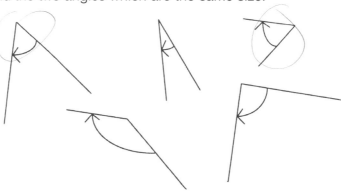

....
1 mark

(b) Draw an angle which is **bigger** than a **right angle**.

1 mark

(c) Kelly is facing **North**.
She turns **clockwise** through **2 right angles**.
Which direction is she facing now?

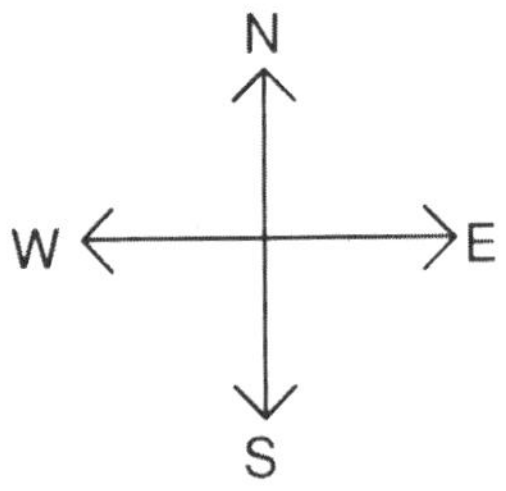

....S....

1 mark

N
↑
W ←———|———→ E
↓
S

(d) Aled is facing **West**.
He turns **clockwise** through **3 right angles**.
Which direction is he facing now?

....S....

1 mark

3 The table shows the distance in miles along the railway line from Shrewsbury to some other stations.

	Miles from Shrewsbury
Shrewsbury	0 miles
Welshpool	20 miles
Newtown	34 miles
Caersws	39 miles
Borth	73 miles
Aberystwyth	82 miles

(a) What is the distance between **Shrewsbury** and **Welshpool**?

20

1 mark

(b) What is the distance between **Welshpool** and **Borth**?

53

1 mark

(c) What is the distance between **Borth** and **Aberystwyth**?

11

1 mark

4 These patterns are from Islamic designs.

Each pattern has one or more lines of symmetry.
Draw **all** the lines of symmetry in each pattern.

You may use a mirror or tracing paper to help you.

Example

....
1 mark

....
1 mark

....
1 mark

THIS IS THE START OF THE TIER 4–6 PAPER

5 (a) These cuboids are made from small cubes.

Write **how many small cubes** there are in each cuboid.

The first is done for you.

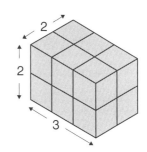

Number of cubes: ....12....

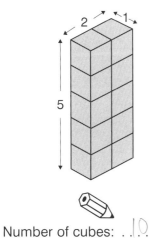

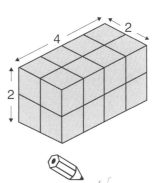

Number of cubes: ..10....

....
1 mark

Number of cubes: ..16.....

....
1 mark

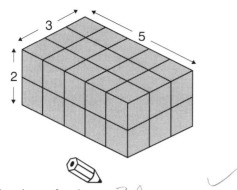

Number of cubes: .3.0. . . . ✓

(b) This shape is made with two cuboids.

Write **how many small cubes** there are in this shape.

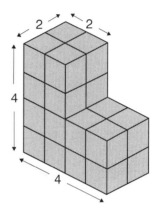

Number of cubes: 24   ✓   16/8/2u

......
1 mark

6 (a) Write what the missing numbers could be in the empty boxes.

  17 +   17 – 10 = 24

......
X
1 mark

 3 × 2 × 5 = 30

......
1 mark

(b) Find the answer.

48 ÷ 4 = 12

......
1 mark

(c) Find the answers.

524 – 249 = 275

......
1 mark

5

46 × 8 =   368

....
1 mark

144 ÷ 9 =   16

....
1 mark

7 (a) A shop sells video tapes for **£2.50** each.
What is the cost of **16** video tapes?

250
6
15.00
25.00
30

£ 30 40

....
1 mark

(b) The shop sells audio cassettes.
Each cassette costs **£1.49**
What is the cost of **4** cassettes?

£ 5.96

....
1 mark

(c) **How many cassettes** can you buy with **£12**?

11.92   8

....
1 mark

(d) The shop also sells cassettes in **packs** of **three**.
A pack costs **£3.99**

How many packs can you buy with **£12**?

3

....
1 mark

Pack of three: £3.99   **Single cassette: £1.49**

(e)   What is the **greatest number** of cassettes you can buy with £15?
You can buy some packs **and** some single cassettes.

11.979
1.49
13.46
1.49
14.95

11

....
1 mark

8   In a magic square, each **row**, **column** and **diagonal** adds up to the same number.

For example, each row, column and diagonal in **this** magic square adds up to **15**

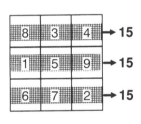

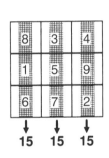

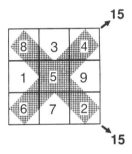

Here is another magic square.

Use the numbers in the first row of this magic square to work out what each row, column and diagonal must add up to.

Then complete the magic square.

24	34	5
2	21	40
37	12	18

24 + 34 + 5 = ...63.

....
1 mark

....
1 mark

....
1 mark

....
1 mark

37
18
55

37
18
19

63
42

63
55

63
20

7

9   Here are the ingredients for **1** fruit cake:

1 fruit cake
200g   self-raising flour
100g   caster sugar
150g   margarine
125g   mixed fruit
3   eggs

(a)   Complete the table to show how much of each ingredient you need to make **10** fruit cakes.

Give your answers in grams **and** in kilograms.

10 fruit cakes

2000 g = 2 kg self-raising flour

1000 g = 1 kg caster sugar

1500 g = 2.5 kg margarine

1250 g = 2.25 kg mixed fruit

30   eggs

1 mark

2 marks

(b)   **6** eggs cost **70p**
How much will **30** eggs cost?

 £ 4.45 3.50

1 mark

THIS IS THE START OF THE TIER 5–7 PAPER

10   A jigsaw has three different sorts of piece.

Corner pieces, with **2** straight sides

Edge pieces with **1** straight side

Middle pieces with **0** straight sides

(a)   This jigsaw has **24** pieces altogether, in **4** rows of **6**.

Complete the table below to show how many of each sort of piece this jigsaw has.

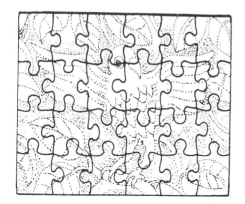

Corner pieces: 4

Edge pieces: 12

Middle pieces: . . . . . 8 . . .

Total: 24

. 1

1 mark

(b)   Another jigsaw has **42** pieces altogether, in **6** rows of **7**.

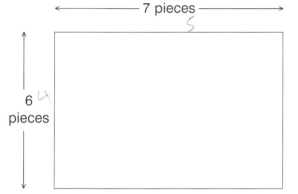

← ——————— 7 pieces ——————— →

5

6 4 pieces

Complete the table below to show how many of each sort of piece this jigsaw has.

Corner pieces: . . . . 4 . . . . .

Edge pieces: . . . 18 . . . . .

Middle pieces: . . 20 . . . . .

Total: 42

. 1

. 1

2 marks

(c)   A **square** jigsaw has **64 middle** pieces.

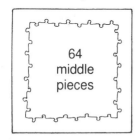

64 middle pieces

Complete the table below to show how many of each sort of piece the **square** jigsaw has, and the total number of pieces.

Remember that the total must be a **square** number.

Corner pieces: . . . . . 4 . . . .

Edge pieces: 24 36

Middle pieces: 64

Total: 92 128

100

X

. . . .

2 marks

11 This is how Caryl works out **15% of 120** in her head.

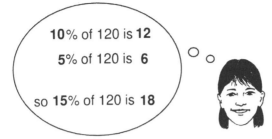

10% of 120 is **12**

5% of 120 is **6**

so **15%** of 120 is **18**

(a) Show how Caryl can work out **17½% of 240** in her head.

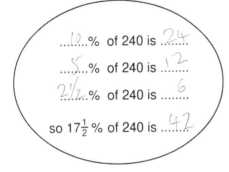

...10..% of 240 is ...24..

...5...% of 240 is ...12...

2½..% of 240 is ....6....

so 17½ % of 240 is ...42..

....
]
....
2 marks

(b) Work out **35% of 520**.
Show your working.

10% 520   52
20%   104
5%   2b
              _____
                182

....
]
....
2 marks

12 (a) A teacher needs **220** booklets.
The booklets are in **packs of 16**.

How many packs must the teacher order?
Show your working.

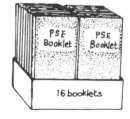

PSE Booklet   PSE Booklet

16 booklets

 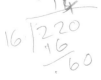

        1⊄
16) 220
     16
     ·60

          3 4
          16
          5 0

.....16.... packs

....

....
2 marks

(b) Each booklet weighs **48g**.

How much do the **220** booklets weigh **altogether**?
Show your working. Give your answer in **kg**.

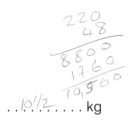

$$\begin{array}{r} 220 \\ 48 \\ \hline 8800 \\ 1760 \\ \hline 10,560 \end{array}$$

. . 10 1/2 . . . . kg

....
....

2 marks

....

1 mark

13 (a) Elin has a bag of marbles.

You cannot see how many marbles are
inside the bag.

Call the number of marbles which Elin
starts with in her bag n.

Elin puts **5 more** marbles **into** her bag.

Write an expression to show the total
number of marbles in Elin's bag now.

$n + 5 = 5^n$

....

1 mark

(b) Ravi has another bag of marbles.

Call the number of marbles which Ravi
starts with in his bag t.

Ravi takes **2 marbles out** of his bag.

Write an expression to show the total
number of marbles in Ravi's bag now.

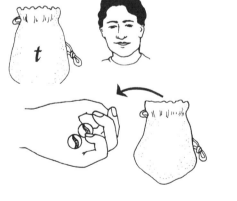

$t - 2 = -2^t$

....

1 mark

(c) Jill has **3** bags of marbles.

Each bag has p marbles inside.

Jill takes some marbles out.

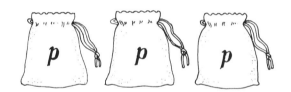

Now the total number of marbles in Jill's 3 bags is $3p - 6$

Some of the statements below **could** be **true**.
Put a tick (✓) by each statement which **could** be **true**.

Jill took **2** marbles out of **one** of the bags, and **none** out of the other bags.	
Jill took **2** marbles out of **each** of the bags.	✓
Jill took **3** marbles out of **one** of the bags, and **none** out of the other bags.	
Jill took **3** marbles out of each of **two** of the bags, and **none** out of the other bag.	
Jill took **6** marbles out of **one** of the bags, and **none** out of the other bags.	
Jill took **6** marbles out of each of **two** of the bags, and **none** out of the other bag.	

....

....

2 marks

14 The pupils in five classes did a quiz.

The following graphs show the scores in each class. Each class had a mean score of 7. In three of the classes, 80% of the pupils got more than the mean score.

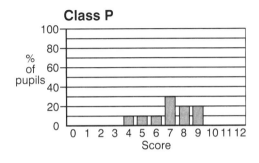

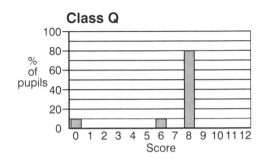

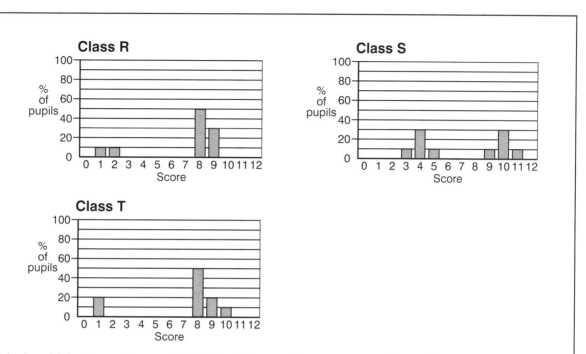

(a)   In which **three** classes did **80%** of the pupils score **more than 7**?

Class . . . .   and   Class . . . .   and   Class . . . .

(b)   Look at the graphs which show that 80% of the pupils scored more than 7.

Some of the statements below are **true** when 80% of the pupils scored more than 7.

Put a tick (✓) by each statement which is **true**.

All of the pupils scored **at least 2**	
Most of the pupils scored **at least 8**	✓
Most of the pupils scored **at least 10**	
Some of the pupils scored **less than 8**	✓

....

....

2 marks

(c) In another quiz the **mean score** was **6**.
Complete this graph to show a mean score of 6.

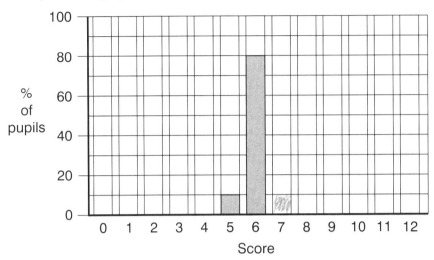

..\.....

1 mark

> **THIS IS THE END OF THE TIER 3–5 PAPER**

> **THIS IS THE START OF THE TIER 6–8 PAPER**

15 Here are five containers:

A   B   C   D   E

 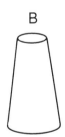   

Water is poured at a constant rate into **three** of the containers.

The graphs show the **depth** of the water as the containers fill up.

graph 1   graph 2   graph 3

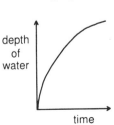   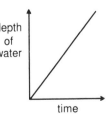   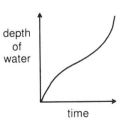

Fill in the gaps below to show which container matches each graph.

Graph 1 matches container . . . . . *B* . . . .

Graph 2 matches container . . . . *C* . . . .

Graph 3 matches container . . . . . *E* . . . .

.... ✗

.... ✗

.... |

3 marks

16 Look at this diagram:

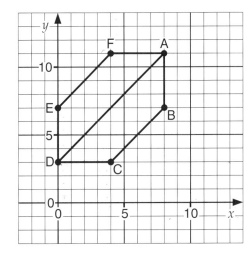

(a) The line through points A and F has the equation $y = 11$
What is the equation of the line through points **A** and **B**?

$E = 6 7$

$X = 8$

.... |

1 mark

(b) The line through points A and D has the equation $y = x + 3$
What is the equation of the line through points **F** and **E**? $y = x + 7$

.... |

1 mark

(c) What is the equation of the line through points **B** and **C**? $y = x + 3$

.... ✗

1 mark

15

17   Each shape in this question has an **area** of **10**cm^2.
No diagram is drawn to scale.

(a)   Calculate the height of the parallelogram.

 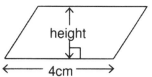

area = 10cm^2 height = ...2-5. . . . cm

. . . .

1 mark

(b)   Calculate the length of the base of the triangle.

 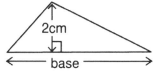

area = 10cm^2 base = ...5. . . . cm   10

. . . .

1 mark

(c)   What might be the values of h, a and b in this trape:
(a is greater than b)

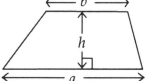

area = 10cm^2 h = ... cm a = ... cm b = ... cm

. . . .

1 mark

What else might the values of h, a and b be?

area = 10cm^2 h = ... cm a = ... cm b = ... cm

. . . .

1 mark

(d)   Look at this rectangle:

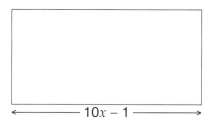

area = 10cm^2

Calculate the value of x and use it to find the length and width of the rectangle.
Show your working.

. . . .

area = 10cm^2 length = ... cm   width = ... cm

. . . .

2 marks

18 This is a series of patterns with grey and white tiles.

The series of patterns continues by adding each time.

pattern number 1

pattern number 2

pattern number 3

12. 20
18. 30
2
3.2
1a

(a) Complete this table:

pattern number	number of **grey** tiles	number of **white** tiles
5	6	10
16	~~18~~ 17	32

....
....
2 marks

(b) Complete this table by writing **expressions**:

pattern number	expression for the number of **grey** tiles	expression for the number of **white** tiles
n	$n + 1$	$2n$

l
....
**
....
2 marks

(c) Write an expression to show the **total** number of tiles in pattern number n.
Simplify your expression.

n^3 $\quad 3n + 1$

....
1 mark

(d) A different series of patterns is made with tiles.

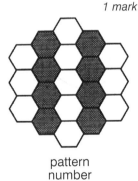

pattern number 1

pattern number 2

pattern number 3

The series of patterns continues by adding 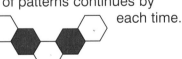 each time.

For this series of patterns, write an expression to show the **total** number of tiles in pattern number n. Show your working and **simplify** your expression.

n

Grey $\quad$ White

$n + 2 \quad\quad 3n$

$5n + 1 + $

....
....
2 marks

19 (a) Each of these calculations has the same answer, **60**
Fill in each gap with a number.

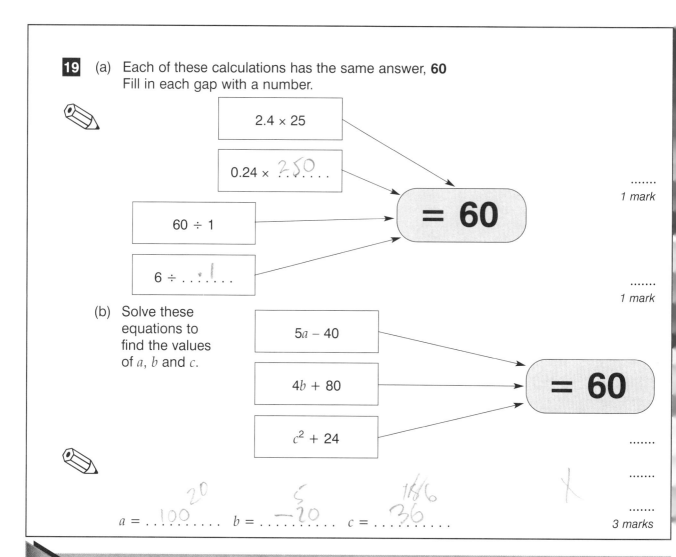

2.4 × 25

0.24 × 250

= 60

....
1 mark

60 ÷ 1

6 ÷ .....1.....

= 60

....
1 mark

(b) Solve these equations to find the values of *a*, *b* and *c*.

5*a* − 40

4*b* + 80

c^2 + 24

= 60

....
....
....

$a = ...100...$ $b = ...−20...$ $c = ...36...$

3 marks

THIS IS THE END OF THE TIER 4–6 PAPER

(c) Solve these simultaneous equations to find the values of *x* and *y*.

x + 8*y*

4*x* − 4*y*

= 60

Show your working.

....

4 × 20 = 80 − 4 × 5 = 20

....

$x = ...20 + 40...$ $y = ...80 − 20...$

....
3 marks

20 In the scale drawing, the shaded area represents a lawn.

There is a wire fence **all around** the lawn.
The shortest distance from the fence to the edge of the lawn is **always 6m**.

On the diagram, draw **accurately** the position of the fence.

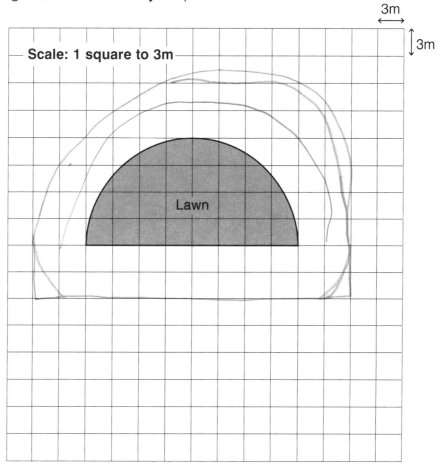

....

....

2 marks

21 This is what a pupil wrote:

> *For all numbers* t *and* w,
>
> $$\frac{1}{t} + \frac{1}{w} = \frac{2}{t + w}$$

Show that the pupil was **wrong**.

....

....

2 marks

19

22   A customer at a supermarket complains to the manager about the waiting times at the checkouts.

The manager records the waiting times of **100 customers** at **1 checkout**.

<u>Results</u>

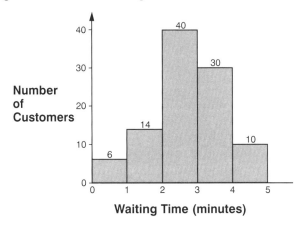

(a) Use the graph to estimate the probability that a customer chosen at random will wait for **2 minutes or longer**.

. . . .

1 mark

(b) Use the graph to estimate the probability that a customer chosen at random will wait for **2.5 minutes or longer**.

. . . .

1 mark

(c) Calculate an estimate of the **mean** waiting time per customer.
Show your working.

You may complete the table below to help you with the calculation.

Waiting Time (minutes)	Mid-point of bar (x)	Number of customers (f)	fx
0 –	0.5	6	3
1 –	1.5	14	
2 –	2.5	40	
3 –	3.5	30	
4 – 5	4.5	10	
		100	

. . . . minutes

....

....

2 marks

(d) The manager wants to improve the survey.
She records the waiting times of more customers.

Give a **different** way the manager could improve the survey.

....
1 mark

23 (a) Find the values of a and b when $p = $ **10**

$a = \dfrac{3p^3}{2}$

$a = \ldots\ldots 90 \ldots\ldots$

....
1 mark

$b = \dfrac{2p^2(p-3)}{7p}$ 40

$b = \ldots\ldots 4 \ldots\ldots$

....
1 mark

(b) Simplify this expression as fully as possible:

$\dfrac{3cd^2}{5cd}$

....
1 mark

> **THIS IS THE END OF THE TIER 5–7 PAPER**

TIER 6–8 ONLY

(c) Multiply out and simplify these expressions:

$3(x - 2) - 2(4 - 3x)$

....
1 mark

$(x + 2)(x + 3)$

....
1 mark

$(x + 4)(x - 1)$

....
1 mark

$(x - 2)^2$

....
1 mark

24 (a) The diagram shows the graph with equation $y = x^2$

On the same axes, sketch the graph with equation $y = 2x^2$

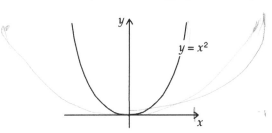

....
1 mark

(b) Curve A is the reflection in the x-axis of $y = x^2$

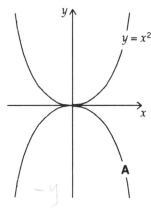

$-x^2 = +y$

What is the equation of curve A?

........$x = y2$......

....
1 mark

(c) Curve B is the translation, one unit up the y-axis, of $y = x^2$

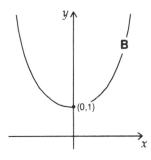

What is the equation of curve B?

. . . .

....
1 mark

(d)   The shaded region is bounded by the curve $y = x^2$ and the line $y = 2$

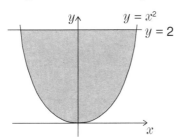

Circle **two** inequalities which together **fully describe** the shaded region.

$y < x^2$ $x < 0$ $y < 2$ $y < 0$

$y > x^2$ $x > 0$ $y > 2$ $y > 0$ ....

....

2 marks

25   (a)   Which of these statements is true? Put a tick (✓) by the correct one.

4×10^3 is a larger number than 4^3 . . . .

4×10^3 is the same size as 4^3 . . . .

4×10^3 is a smaller number than 4^3 . . . .

Explain your answer.

....

1 mark

(b)   One of the numbers below has the same value as **3.6×10^4**
       Put a tick (✓) under the correct number.

36^3 36^4 $(3.6 \times 10)^4$ 0.36×10^3 0.36×10^5

. . . .

....

1 mark

(c) One of the numbers below has the same value as **2.5 × 10⁻³**
Put a tick (✓) under the correct number.

25×10^{-4} 2.5×10^{3} -2.5×10^{3} 0.00025   2500

....

....
1 mark

(d) $(2 \times 10^2) \times (2 \times 10^2)$ can be written more simply as 4×10^4

Write these values as simply as possible:

$(3 \times 10^2) \times (2 \times 10^{-2})$

....
1 mark

$$\frac{6 \times 10^8}{2 \times 10^4}$$

....
1 mark

26   100 students were asked whether they studied French or German.

Results:

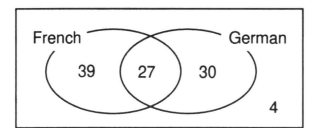

27 students studies both French **and** German.

(a) What is the probability that a student chosen at random will study only **one** of the languages?

....
1 mark

(b) What is the probability that a student who is studying German is also studying French?

....

1 mark

(c) Two of the 100 students are chosen at random.

Circle the calculation which shows the probability that **both** students study French and German.

$$\frac{27}{100} \times \frac{26}{100} \qquad\qquad \frac{27}{100} + \frac{26}{99} \qquad\qquad \frac{27}{100} + \frac{27}{100}$$

....

1 mark

$$\frac{27}{100} \times \frac{26}{99} \qquad\qquad \frac{27}{100} \times \frac{27}{100}$$

27   This shape is designed using 3 semi-circles.

The radii of the semi-circles are $3a$, $2a$ and a.

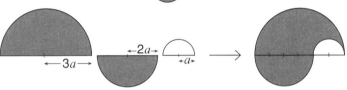

(a) Find the area of each semi-circle, in terms of a and π, and show that the **total** area of the shape is $6\pi a^2$.

....

....

....

3 marks

(b) The area, $6\pi a^2$, of the shape is 12cm^2.
Write an equation in the form of $a = \ldots$, leaving your answer in terms of π.
Show your working and **simplify** your equation.

....

....

2 marks

THIS IS THE END OF THE TIER 6–8 PAPER

Paper 2

THIS IS THE START OF THE TIER 3–5 PAPER

1 Dan is doing a sponsored swim.

This is what Dan's friends promise to give for each length of the swimming pool he swims.

Calculators
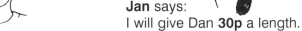
You **may** use a calculator to answer any question in this test if you want to.

Ben says:
I will give Dan **20p** a length.

Cal says:
I will give Dan **25p** a length.

Jan says:
I will give Dan **30p** a length.

Kim says:
I will give Dan **15p** a length.

Wyn says:
I will give Dan **20p** a length.

(a) Fill in the gaps in Dan's sponsor form.

Name	Amount for each length
Ben	20p
Cal	25
Jan	30p
Kim	15p
Wyn	20p

....
....
2 marks

(b) How much money will Dan collect altogether for each length he swims?

£ 1.10

....
1 mark

(c) Tom also did the sponsored swim. He swam **27** lengths.
He collected **75p** for each length.

How much money did Tom collect for the swim?

£ 20.25

....
1 mark

(d) Nina swam **25** lengths in the sponsored swim.
She collected **72p** for each length.
How much money did Nina collect for the swim?

£ 18

....
1 mark

Nina's mother says:

Tell me how much you collected for your swim.
I will give you a **quarter** of the amount.

How much should Nina's mother give her?

£ 4.50

....
1 mark

2 Look at the pictures of
Japanese money.

1000   100   10   1
YEN   YEN   YEN   YEN

Write how much is in each box.
The first is done for you.

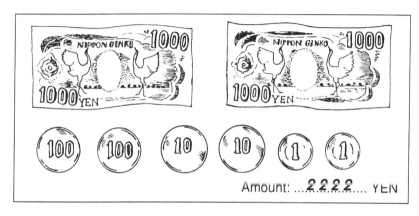

Amount: ...*2222*.... YEN

27

(a)

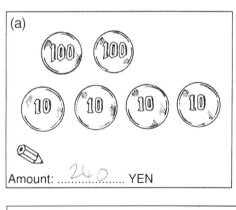

Amount: ...240... YEN

(b)

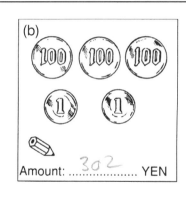

Amount: ...302... YEN

....
1 mark

....
1 mark

(c)

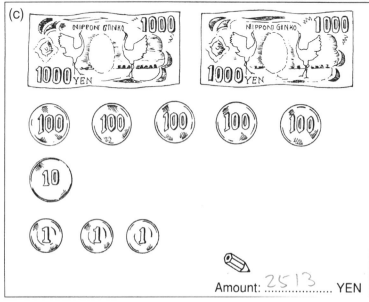

Amount: ...2513... YEN

....
1 mark

(d)

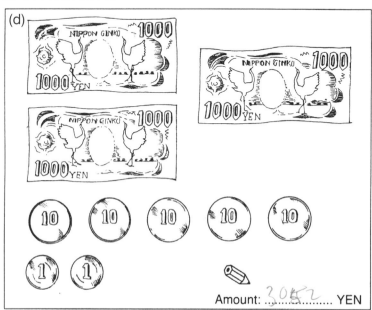

Amount: ...3052... YEN

....
1 mark

3 **2 boxes** balance **1 can**.   **2 cans** balance **1 bottle**.

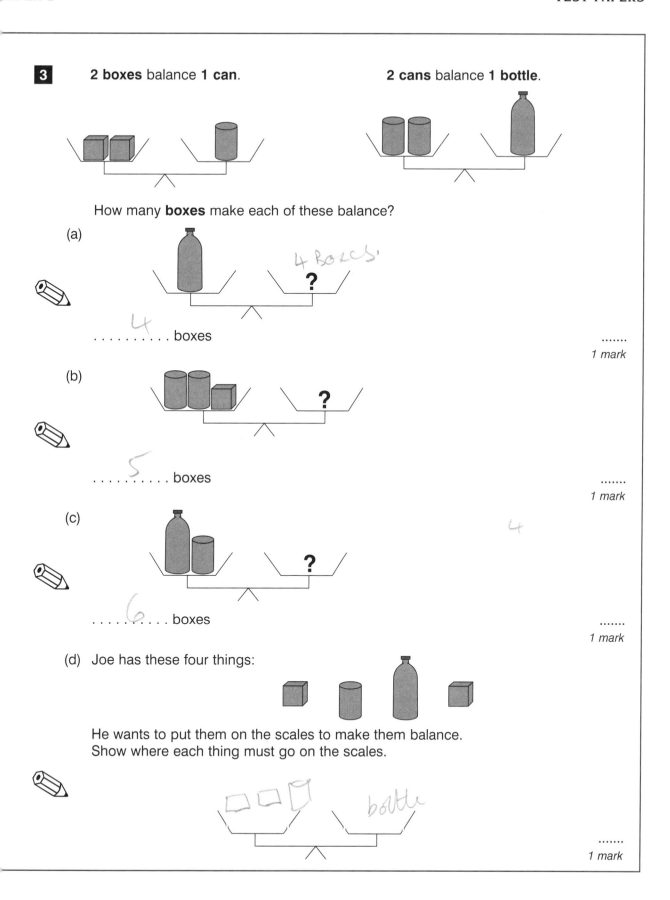

How many **boxes** make each of these balance?

(a)

4 Boxes!

. . . . 4 . . . boxes

....
1 mark

(b)

. . . . 5 . . . boxes

....
1 mark

(c)

4

. . . . . 6 . . . boxes

....
1 mark

(d) Joe has these four things:

He wants to put them on the scales to make them balance.
Show where each thing must go on the scales.

bottle

....
1 mark

4   Look at the calendar for the first four months in 1998.
Monday, February 16 is shaded on the calendar.

	January				February			
Sunday	4	11	18	25	1	8	15	22
Monday	5	12	19	26	2	9	16	23
Tuesday	6	13	20	27	3	10	17	24
Wednesday	7	14	21	28	4	11	18	25
Thursday	1	8	15	22	29	5	12	19	26
Friday	2	9	16	23	30	6	13	20	27
Saturday	3	10	17	24	31	7	14	21	28

	March					April			
Sunday	1	8	15	22	29		5	12	19	26
Monday	2	9	16	23	30		6	13	20	27
Tuesday	3	10	17	24	31		7	14	21	28
Wednesday	4	11	18	25		1	8	15	22	29
Thursday	5	12	19	26		2	9	16	23	30
Friday	6	13	20	27		3	10	17	24	
Saturday	7	14	21	28		4	11	18	25	

(a)   What was the date of the **third Sunday** in **January**?

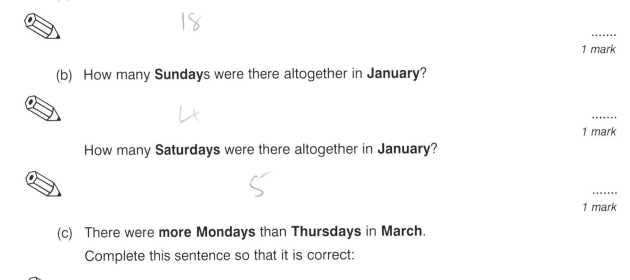

18

....
1 mark

(b)   How many **Sunday**s were there altogether in **January**?

4

....
1 mark

How many **Saturdays** were there altogether in **January**?

5

....
1 mark

(c)   There were **more Mondays** than **Thursdays** in **March**.

Complete this sentence so that it is correct:

There were more .....Thursd..... than ...Mond...in **April**.

....
1 mark

(d) Jane went swimming on **Wednesday, January 14**.
She went swimming again **4 weeks later**.
On **what date** did she go swimming the second time?

11 Feb.

....
1 mark

(e) The swimming pool **shut** for repairs on **Friday, March 20**.
It **opened** again on **Friday, April 10**.
For **how many weeks** was the swimming pool shut?

3 weeks.

....
1 mark

(f) Which day in **March** had numbers in the **7 times table** as its dates?

Sat

....
1 mark

THIS IS THE START OF THE TIER 4–6 PAPER

5   Owen has some tiles like these:

He uses the tiles to make a series of patterns.

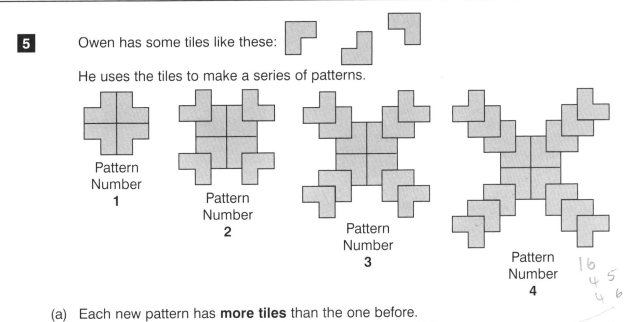

Pattern
Number
1

Pattern
Number
2

Pattern
Number
3

Pattern
Number
4

(a) Each new pattern has **more tiles** than the one before.
The number of tiles goes up by the same amount each time.
How many **more** tiles does Owen add each time he makes a new pattern?

4

1 mark

31

(b) **How many tiles** will Owen need altogether to make **pattern number 6**?

24

....
1 mark

(c) **How many tiles** will Owen need altogether to make **pattern number 9**?

36

....
1 mark

(d) Owen uses **40 tiles** to make a pattern.
What is the **number** of the **pattern** he makes?

10

....
1 mark

6 Here are four spinners, labelled P, Q, R and S.

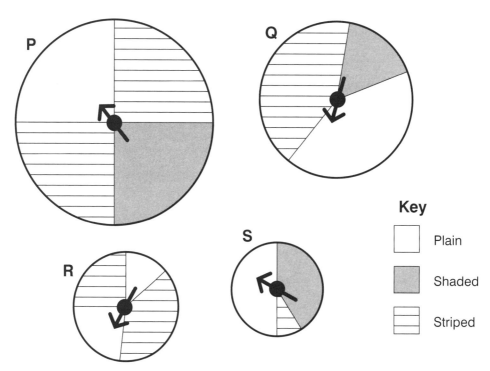

(a) Which spinner gives the **greatest chance** that the arrow will land on **plain**?

Spinner . . . .

....

1 mark

(b) Which spinner gives the **smallest chance** that the arrow will land on **shaded**?

Spinner . . . .

....

1 mark

(c) Shade this spinner so that it is **certain** that the arrow will land on **shaded**.

....

1 mark

(d) Shade this spinner so that there is a **50% chance** that the arrow will land on **shaded**.

....

1 mark

7   Jim, Bob, Liz and Meg had a games competition.

They played two games, Draughts and Ludo.

Each pupil played each of the others at the two different games.

Meg recorded **how many** games each person won.

Jim	/ / /
Meg	/ / /
Liz	/ / / /
Bob	/ /

Jim recorded **who won** each game.

Draughts	Ludo
Jim	Meg
Liz	Bob
Bob	
Jim	Meg
Jim	Liz
Liz	Meg

(a)   Jim forgot to put one of the names on his table.
Use Meg's table to work out what the missing name is.

Liz

.... *1 mark*

(b)   Who won the **most** games of **Draughts**?

Jim

.... *1 mark*

(c)   Give one reason why **Meg's** table is a good way of recording the results.

Only 3 games

✗ .... *1 mark*

(d)   Give one reason why **Jim's** table is a good way of recording the results.

Only 3 games.

✗ .... *1 mark*

THIS IS THE START OF THE TIER 5–7 PAPER

8 The table shows the length of some rivers to the nearest km.

(a) Write the length of each river rounded to the nearest **100km**.

River	Length in km to the nearest km	Length in km to the nearest 100km
Severn	354	400
Thames	346	300
Trent	297	300
Wye	215	200
Dee	113	100

1 mark

Which two rivers have the **same length** to the nearest **100km**?

.....Thames and .....Trent

1 mark

(b) Write the length of each river rounded to the nearest **10km**.

River	Length in km to the nearest km	Length in km to the nearest 10km
Severn	354	350
Thames	346	350
Trent	297	300
Wye	215	220
Dee	113	110

1 mark

Which two rivers have the **same length** to the nearest **10km**?

.....Severn and .....Thames.

1 mark

35

(c) There is another river which is not on the list.

It has a length of **200km** to the **nearest 100km**,
and a length of **150km** to the **nearest 10km**.

Complete this sentence to give one possible length of the river to the nearest km.

The length of the river could be . . 1 5 4 . . . km.

.)......

1 mark

(d) Two more rivers have **different** lengths to the nearest km.

They both have a length of **250km** to the **nearest 10km**,
but their lengths to the **nearest 100km** are **different**.

Complete this sentence to give a possible length of each river to the nearest km.

The lengths of the rivers could be . . . . 254 km and . . 246 . . km.   ...|....

.|......

2 marks

9 These two congruent triangles
make a **parallelogram**.

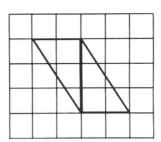

(a) Draw another
congruent triangle
to make a **rectangle**.

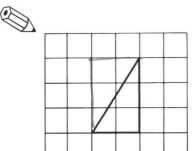

....

1 mark

TIERS 3–5 & 4–6 ONLY

TIERS 3–5 & 4–6 ONLY

(b) Draw another congruent triangle to make a **bigger triangle**.

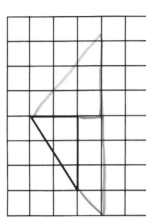

(c) Draw another congruent triangle to make a **different bigger triangle**.

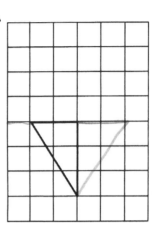

......|......
1 mark

......|.......
1 mark

10 You can make different colours of paint by mixing red, blue and yellow in different **proportions**.

For example, you can make green by mixing **1 part blue** to **1 part yellow**.

(a) To make purple, you mix **3 parts red** to **7 parts blue**.

How much of each colour do you need to make **20 litres** of purple paint?

Give your answer in litres.

. . . . . . 6 . . . litres of red   and   . . . . . 14 . . . . litres of blue

..|.....

....
2 marks

13/m   7/mt.

(b) To make orange, you mix **13 parts yellow** to **7 parts red**.

How much of each colour do you need to make **10 litres** of orange paint?

Give your answer in litres.

. . . . 6.5 . . litres of red   and   . . . . . . 3.5 . . litres of yellow

|
....

|
,,,,,,,
2 marks

37

11 This shape is called an **L-triomino**. It is made from three squares.

This shape is made from two L-triominoes. They do not overlap. It has only **one line** of symmetry.

You may use a mirror or tracing paper to help you in this question.

(a) Draw a **different** shape made from two L-triominoes which do not overlap. It must have only **one line** of symmetry.

....
1 mark

(b) Draw a shape made from two L-triominoes which do not overlap. It must have **two lines** of symmetry.

....
1 mark

This shape is made from two
L-triominoes which do not overlap.

It has **rotational** symmetry of
order **two**.

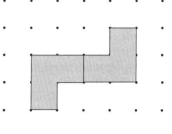

(c) Draw a **different** shape made from two L-triominoes which do not overlap.
It must have **rotational** symmetry of order **two**.

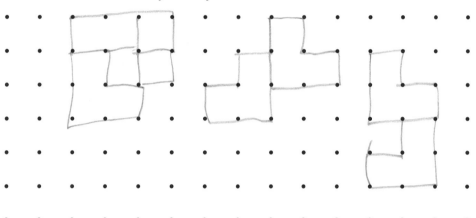

1 mark

(d) Draw a shape made from two L-triominoes which do not overlap.
It must have **two** lines of symmetry **and rotational** symmetry of order **two**.

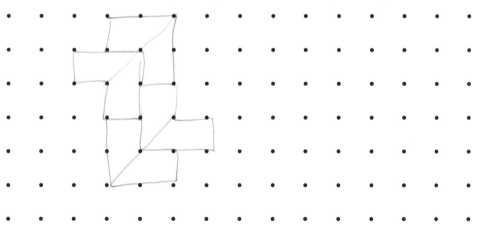

1 mark

12 These pie charts show some information about the ages of people in Greece and in Ireland.

There are about 10 million people in Greece, and there are about 3.5 million people in Ireland.

Greece

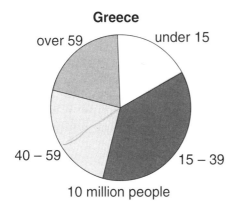

10 million people

Ireland

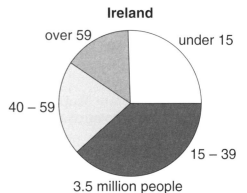

3.5 million people

(a) Roughly what **percentage** of people in **Greece** are aged **40–59**?

.....30.....%

....
1 mark

(b) There are about **10 million** people in Greece.
Use your percentage from part (a) to work out roughly **how many** people in Greece are aged **40–59**.

...3....... million people

....
1 mark

(c) Dewi says:

> The charts show that there are **more** people **under 15** in **Ireland** than in **Greece**.

Dewi is **wrong**. Explain why the charts do **not** show this.

only 3.5 mil against 10 mil.

....
1 mark

40

(d) There are about 60 million people in the UK.
The table shows roughly what percentage of people in the UK are of different ages.

under 15	15 – 39	40 – 59	over 59
20%	35%	25%	20%

Draw a pie chart below, right to show the information in the table.

Label each section of your pie chart clearly with the **ages**.

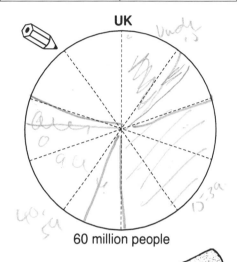

UK

60 million people

....

....

2 marks

....

1 mark

13 (a) The top and the base of this box are **semi-circles**.

One of the nets below could fold up to make a box like this.

Put a tick (✓) on the correct net.

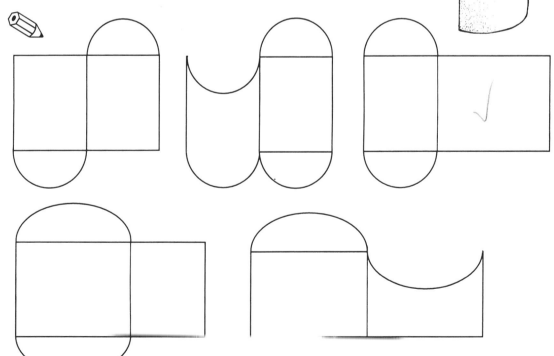

....

1 mark

41

(b) This is a rough sketch of the **base** of a box.
It is a **semi-circle**, with **diameter 8cm.**

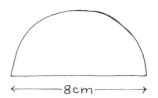

←————8cm————→

Make an accurate, full size drawing of the **base** of the box.

You will need a ruler and a pair of compasses.

....

....

2 marks

THIS IS THE END OF THE TIER 3–5 PAPER

THIS IS THE START OF THE TIER 6–8 PAPER

14   I have two fair dice.
Each of the dice is numbered 1 to 6.

(a) The probability that I will throw **double 6**
(both dice showing number 6) is

$$\frac{1}{36}$$

What is the probability that I will **not** throw double 6?

$$\frac{36}{1}$$

....

1 mark

(b) I throw both dice and get double 6.
Then I throw the dice again.

Tick the box that describes the probability that I will throw **double 6** this time.

less than $\frac{1}{36}$ ☐

$\frac{1}{36}$ ☑

more than $\frac{1}{36}$ ☐

Explain your answer.

Because all the chances are even for every number.

....

1 mark

I start again and throw both dice.

(c) What is the probability that I will throw **double 3** (both dice showing number 3)?

$\frac{1}{36}$

....

1 mark

(d) What is the probability that I will throw a double?
(It could be double 1 or double 2 or any other double.)

$\frac{1}{36}$

....

1 mark

15 The table shows the land area of each of the World's continents.

continent	land area (in 1000km^2)
Africa	30 264
Antarctica	13 209
Asia	44 250
Europe	9 907
North America	24 398
Oceania	8 534
South America	17 793
World	**148 355**

(a) Which continent is approximately 12% of the World's land area?

South America

....

....
1 mark

(b) What percentage of the World's land area is **Antarctica**?
Show your working.

14 83

.... 9 ....%

....
....
2 marks

(c) About **30%** of the World's area is **land**. The rest is water.
The amount of **land** in the World is about **150 million km^2**.

Work out the approximate **total area** (land and water) of the World.
Show your working.

....500.... million km^2

....
....
2 marks

Data from *Book of Comparisons* pub. Penguin 1980

TIERS 5–7 & 6–8 ONLY

16   Four cubes join to make an L-shape.

The diagram shows the L-shape after **quarter turns** in one direction.

On the paper below, draw the L-shape after
the **next** quarter turn in the same direction.

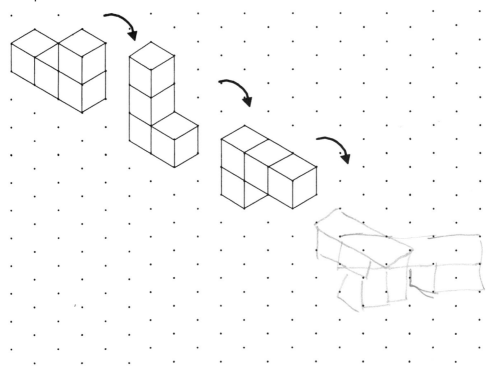

....

....
2 marks

17   A competition has 3 different games.

(a)   Jeff plays 2 of the games.

	Game A	Game B	Game C
Score	62	53	65

To win, Jeff needs a **mean** score of **60**.
How many points does he need to score in Game C?
Show your working.

....

. . . .

....

57

2 marks

45

(b) Imran and Nia play the 3 games.

Their scores have the **same mean**.
The **range** of Imran's scores is **twice** the range of Nia's scores.

Fill in the missing scores in the table below:

Imran's scores	.....40....	40	..40......
Nia's scores	35	40	45

....
1 mark

The scatter diagrams show the scores of everyone who plays all 3 games.

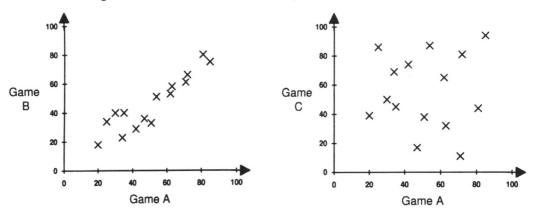

(c) Look at the scatter diagrams.
Which statement most closely describes the **relationship** between the games?

Tick (✓) the correct statement.

Game **A** and Game **B**				
perfect negative relationship	negative relationship	no relationship	positive relationship	perfect positive relationship
			✓	

....
1 mark

Game **A** and Game **C**				
perfect negative relationship	negative relationship	no relationship	positive relationship	perfect positive relationship
		✓		

....
1 mark

(d) What can you tell about the **relationship** between the scores on Game **B** and the scores on Game **C**?

Tick (✓) the statement that most closely describes the relationship.

Game **B** and Game **C**				
perfect negative relationship	negative relationship	no relationship	positive relationship	perfect positive relationship
		✓		

.... *1 mark*

18 A box for coffee is in the shape of a hexagagonal prism.

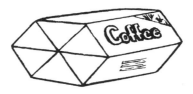

One end of the box is shown below.

Each of the 6 triangles in the hexagon has the same dimensions.

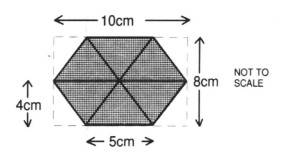

NOT TO SCALE

(a) Calculate the total **area** of the hexagon.
Show your working.

8×7.5

6.1

60

$\times\ 60$

..1600.. cm²

....
.... *2 marks*

(b) The box is **10cm long**.

After packing, the coffee fills **80%** of the box.

How many **grams** of coffee are in the box?
(The mass of 1cm^3 of coffee is 0.5 grams.)

Show your working.

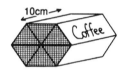

. . . . grams   3 marks

THIS IS THE END OF THE TIER 4–6 PAPER

TIERS 5–7 & 6–8 ONLY

(c) A **227g** packet of the same coffee costs **£2.19**

How much **per 100g** of coffee is this?

Show your working.

£. . . . .   2 marks

48

19 At Winchester there is a large table known as the Round Table of King Arthur.

The **diameter** of the table is **5.5 metres**.

(a) A book claims that 50 people sat round the table.

Assume each person needs 45cm around the circumference of the table.
Is it possible for 50 people to sit around the table?

Show your working to explain your answer.

$$\pi \times D = \frac{17.27m}{.45} = 38 \quad \therefore No!$$

....
....
....

3 marks

(b) Assume people sitting around the table could reach only **1.5m**.

Calculate the **area** of the table that could be reached.

Show your working.

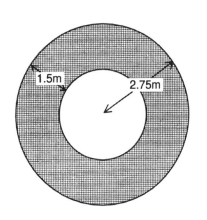

1.5m   2.75m

. . . . m²   *3 marks*

20 Some pupils threw 3 fair dice.

They recorded how many times the numbers on the dice were the same.

Name	Number of throws	Results		
		all different	2 the same	all the same
Morgan	40	26	12	2
Sue	140	81	56	3
Zenta	20	10	10	0
Ali	100	54	42	4

(a) Write the name of the pupil whose data are **most likely** to give the best estimate of the probability of getting each result.

Explain your answer.

....
1 mark

(b) This table shows the pupils' results collected together:

Number of throws	Results		
	all different	2 the same	all the same
300	171	120	9

Use these data to estimate the **probability** of throwing numbers that are **all different**.

....
1 mark

(c) The theoretical probability of each result is shown below:

	all different	2 the same	all the same
Probability	$\dfrac{5}{9}$	$\dfrac{5}{12}$	$\dfrac{1}{36}$

Use these probabilities to calculate, for 300 throws, **how many times** you would theoretically expect to get each result.

Number	Theoretical results		
of throws	all different	2 the same	all the same
300	. . . .	. . . .	. . . .

....

....

2 marks

(d) Explain why the pupils' results are not the same as the theoretical results.

....

1 mark

(e) Jenny throws the 3 dice twice.

Calculate the probability that she gets **all the same** on her first throw and gets **all the same** on her second throw.

Show your working.

....

....

2 marks

21 In this question you will get no marks if you work out the answer through scale drawing.

(a) Cape Point is 7.5km east and 4.8km north of Arton.

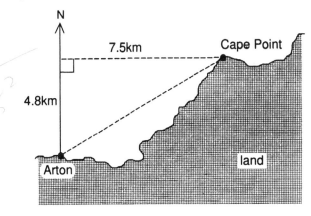

$4.8^2 + 7.5^2$

NOT TO SCALE

Calculate the direct distance from Arton to Cape Point.
Show your working.

23.04
56.25
$\sqrt{79.29}$

8.9Km

....
....
2 marks

. . . 9.9 . . . km

Bargate is 6km east and 4km north of Cape Point.

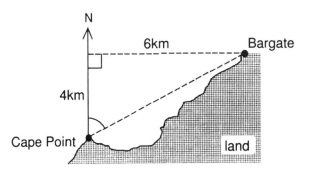

NOT TO SCALE

(b) Steve wants to sail directly from Cape Point to Bargate.
On what bearing should he sail?

Show your working.

....

....

. . . . °   *2 marks*

(c) Anna sails from Cape Point on a bearing of 048°.
She stops when she is due north of Bargate.

How far north of Bargate is Anna?
Show your working.

....

....

....

. . . . km   *3 marks*

22 Look at the table:

Birth rate per 1000 population

	1961	1994
England	17.6	
Wales	17.0	12.2

(a) In England, from 1961 to 1994, the birth rate **fell** by 26.1%.
What was the birth rate in England in 1994?

Show your working.

....

....

. . . .   *2 marks*

(b) In Wales, the birth rate also fell.
     Calculate the **percentage fall** from 1961 to 1994.

     Show your working.

....

....

. . . . %

2 marks

> **THIS IS THE END OF THE TIER 5–7 PAPER**

TIER 6–8 ONLY

(c) From 1961 to 1994, the birth rates in Scotland and Northern Ireland fell by the **same** amount.

The **percentage fall** in Scotland was greater than the percentage fall in Northern Ireland.

Put a tick (✓) by the statement below which is true.

In 1961, the birth rate in Scotland was **higher** than the birth rate in Northern Ireland.	. . . .
In 1961, the birth rate in Scotland was **the same as** the birth rate in Northern Ireland.	. . . .
In 1961, the birth rate in Scotland was **lower** than the birth rate in Northern Ireland.	. . . .
From the information given, you cannot tell whether Scotland or Northern Ireland had the higher birth rate in 1961.	. . . .

....

1 mark

23 The cumulative frequency graph shows the height of 150 Norway fir trees.

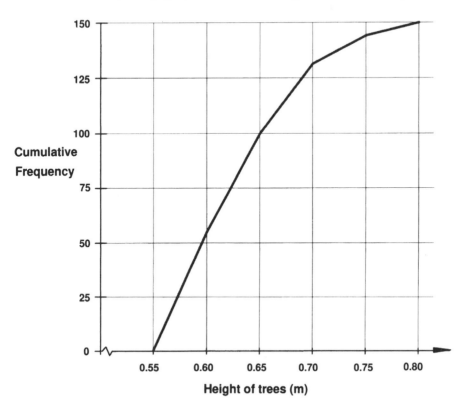

(a) Use the graph to estimate the **median** height and the **interquartile range** of the Norway firs.

median = ... m

....
1 mark

....

....

interquartile range = ... m

2 marks

(b) One of these sketches shows the distribution of heights of the Norway firs.
     Put a tick (✓) by the side of the correct frequency diagram.

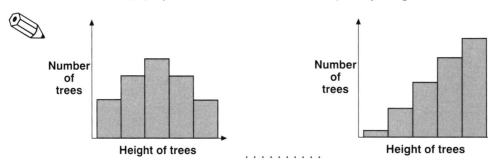

. . . .

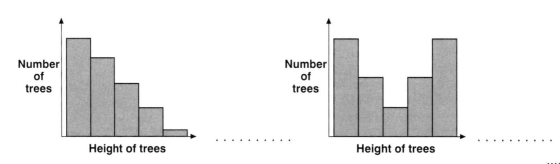

. . . .

....

1 mark

24 These plant pots are mathematically similar.
     The internal dimensions are shown.

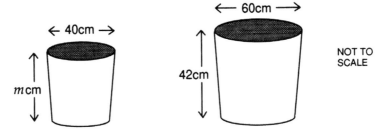

NOT TO
SCALE

(a) Calculate the value of m.
     Show your working.

....

....

$m = $ . . . . cm   *2 marks*

(b) The capacity, C, of a plant pot in **cubic centimetres** is given by the formula:

$$C = \frac{1}{12}\pi h(a^2 + ab + b^2)$$

In the larger plant pot $a = 60$, $b = 36$ and $h = 42$
How many **litres** of compost are needed to fill the plant pot?

Show your working.

....

....

....

. . . . litres   *3 marks*

(c) Think about the ratio of the widths of the two plant pots.

Explain why the ratio of the capacity of the smaller pot to the capacity of the larger pot is **8 : 27**.

....

1 mark

THIS IS THE END OF THE TIER 6–8 PAPER

Mental arithmetic test C (Lower tier)

"For this first group of questions you will have 5 seconds to work out each answer and write it down."

	The Questions:
1	Imagine two squares that are the same size. Imagine you join them together side by side. What is the name of the new shape you have made? *Rectangle*
2	Write the number two thousand and twenty-eight in figures. *2028*
3	How many centimetres are there in one metre? *1000 mm*
4	Write a number that is bigger than twenty-eight and a half but less than twenty-nine. *28 3/4*
5	What is nine multiplied by seven? *56*
6	Look at the equation on your answer sheet. What is the value of two y?
7	What is seven hundred and thirty-two divided by one hundred? *73.2*

"For the next group of questions you will have 10 seconds to work out each answer and write it down."

	The Questions:
8	What is the cost of four birthday cards at one pound and five pence each? *6.00*
9	Your answer sheet shows three scores in a darts game. What is the total score?
10	Look at the spinners on your answer sheet. Tick the spinner which is most likely to land on grey.
11	Look at the equation on your answer sheet. What is the value of n?
12	What number is one hundred less than eight thousand? Write your answer in figures. *7900*
13	The pie chart on your answer sheet shows how a group of pupils travel to school. Approximately what percentage of these pupils cycle to school?
14	Look at the squares on your answer sheet. How many small squares will fit inside the larger square?
15	A jacket costs fifty-two pounds. In a sale the price is nineteen pounds less. What is the sale price?

	The Questions:
16	A pen costs three pounds forty-nine. I buy two pens. How much change do I get from ten pounds?
17	How many hours is three hundred minutes?
18	Subtract twenty from eight.
19	The perimeter of an equilateral triangle is thirty centimetres. What is the length of each side?
20	A famous author lived in a house from eighteen eighty-seven to nineteen twenty. For how long did she live there?
21	Look at the calculation on your answer sheet. Work out the answer.
22	Look at the measurements on your answer sheet. Which one is about the same length as five miles? Circle your answer.
23	A skirt cost thirty pounds. The price went up by ten per cent. What is the new price?

"For the next group of questions you will have 15 seconds to work out each answer and write it down."

	The Questions:
24	One of the shapes on your answer sheet has no lines of symmetry. Put a tick inside this shape.
25	Look at the timetable on your answer sheet. How long does the journey take from Tarn to Barham?
26	Imagine a square, cut out of paper. Put a ring around two shapes you could make by folding the square in half.
27	Look at the numbers on your answer sheet. Put a circle around the smallest number.
28	Use the calculation on your answer sheet to help you work out the answer to one hundred and forty-four divided by six.
29	Imagine a solid cone, standing on its circular base. Cut the cone in half, from top to bottom. What is the shape of the vertical face made by the cut?
30	What is the next prime number after twenty-three?

5 2/9
1 9
3 3

Mental arithmetic test A (Higher tiers)

"For this first group of questions you will have 5 seconds to work out each answer and write it down."

	The Questions:
1	What is thirty-seven multiplied by ten?
2	Write one quarter as a decimal.
3	There are four red cubes and six blue cubes in a bag. I choose a cube at random. What is the probability that I choose a blue cube?
4	How many metres are there in two and a half kilometres?

"For the next group of questions you will have 10 seconds to work out each answer and write it down."

	The Questions:
5	Look at the calculation on your answer sheet. Work out the answer.
6	What is five point four added to three point seven?
7	Twenty-five per cent of a number is twelve. What is the number?
8	Look at the expression on your answer sheet. Its value is eighty-two. Write an expression with a value of forty-one.
9	Write another fraction that is equivalent to three-fifths.
10	Look at the triangle on your answer sheet. What is the area of this triangle?
11	Look at the equation on your answer sheet. If m equals six, what is h?
12	Look at the equation on your answer sheet. Write what number x could be.
13	Look at the equation on your answer sheet. What is the value of n?
14	In a country, the probability that it will rain in August is nought point nought five. What is the probability that it will not rain in August?
15	Assume a person's heart beats seventy times in one minute. How many times will it beat in one hour?
16	The mean of a, b, and c is ten. a is six. b is eleven. What is c?

	The Questions:
17	Look at the expression on your answer sheet. Multiply out this expression.
18	Write an approximate answer to the calculation on your answer sheet.

"For the next group of questions you will have 15 seconds to work out each answer and write it down."

	The Questions:
19	Arrange the digits three, five and two to make the largest possible odd number.
20	Look at the lengths on your answer sheet. Put a circle around the median length.
21	Use the calculation on your answer sheet to help you work out the answer to fourteen multiplied by three point nine.
22	What is eighteen multiplied by nine?
23	Imagine a robot moving so that it is always the same distance from a fixed point. Describe the shape of the path the robot makes.
24	Two of the angles in a triangle are forty-seven degrees and eighty-five degrees. How many degrees is the other angle?
25	The sum of p and q is twelve. The product of p and q is twenty-seven. What are the values of p and q?
26	Seventy-five miles per hour is about the same as thirty-three metres per second. About how many metres per second is fifty miles per hour?
27	Look at the net of a cube on your answer sheet. When you fold it up, which edge will meet edge A? Draw an arrow pointing to the correct edge.
28	In a raffle, one half of the tickets are bought by men. One third are bought by women. The rest are bought by children. What fraction of the tickets are bought by children?
29	Multiply twenty-five by twenty-eight.
30	A cuboid has edges of three, four and five centimetres. Its volume is sixty cubic centimetres. What is the volume of a cuboid with edges that are twice as long?

Mental arithmetic test B (Higher tiers)

"For this first group of questions you will have 5 seconds to work out each answer and write it down."

	The Questions:
1	What is sixty-three divided by nine?
2	How many millilitres are there in a litre?
3	A quarter of a number is one point two five. What is the number?
4	I throw two dice. The probability that I get a total of eight is five thirty-sixths. What is the probability that I do not get a total of eight?

"For the next group of questions you will have 10 seconds to work out each answer and write it down."

	The Questions:
5	I spend two pounds twenty. How much change will I get from five pounds?
6	Look at the measurements on your answer sheet. Which one is about the same length as one metre? Circle your answer.
7	Pencils cost thirty-seven pence each. How many pencils can you buy with three pounds seventy?
8	Two angles fit together to make a straight line. One angle is eighty-six degrees. How many degrees is the other angle?
9	Thirty-five per cent of a number is forty-two. What is seventy per cent of the number?
10	Look at the cuboid on your answer sheet. What is the volume of this cuboid?
11	Four out of fifty pupils were absent from school. What percentage of pupils were absent?
12	What is five point one multiplied by one thousand?
13	Imagine a regular square-based pyramid. Imagine another identical pyramid. Stick their square faces together. How many faces does your new shape have?
14	Look at the calculation on your answer sheet. Write down the answer.
15	Rearrange the equation on your answer sheet to make b the subject of the equation.

	The Questions:
16	Write in figures the number that is one less than seven and a half million.
17	Imagine two trees. Now imagine walking so that you are always an equal distance from each tree. Describe the shape of the path that you walk.
18	The probability that a train will be late is nought point three. Of fifty trains, about how many would you expect to be late?

"For the next group of questions you will have 15 seconds to work out each answer and write it down."

	The Questions:
19	Look at the dots on your answer sheet. Four of the dots are at the corners of a square. Join the four dots to make a square.
20	The pie chart on your answer sheet shows how two hundred pupils travel to school. Roughly how many of these pupils cycle to school?
21	What is one hundred and twenty-eight multiplied by five?
22	Use the calculation on your answer sheet to help you work out the answer to four hundred and sixty-eight divided by fifteen.
23	Estimate the value of five hundred and two divided by forty-nine.
24	Carpet tiles are fifty centimetres by fifty centimetres. How many do you need to cover one square metre?
25	Look at the equation on your answer sheet. If c equals eight, what is d?
26	A square has an area of t squared. What is the perimeter of the square?
27	x equals two and y equals three. Work out the value of x to the power y plus y to the power x.
28	Look at the calculation on your answer sheet. Write an approximate answer.
29	Look at the equation on your answer sheet. Write an expression, in terms of t, for m plus five.
30	On your answer sheet are two numbers. Write the number which is halfway between them.

Paper 1

THIS IS THE START OF THE TIER 3–5 PAPER

Question 1

Part	Mark	Answer	Tutorial	What's this question looking for?
(a)	1 1	9:15 45 minutes	• You can indicate the first answer in several ways e.g. 09 15, 9:15, 9:15 a.m, 9:15 p.m., quarter past nine and so on. • The second part asks for an answer in minutes, although 45 minutes can be written as 'three-quarters of an hour' etc. • Questions about time are quite common on SATs. They are set in the non-calculator paper because you cannot use an ordinary calculator to solve time problems. Working out 915 – 830 on a calculator gives an answer of 85. This is not the answer you want, because there are not 100 minutes in an hour. You have to count on to the hour and then count past the hour. It helps to think of the answer like this 7:00 7:15 7:30 7:45 8:00 8:15 8:30 8:45 9:00 9:15 9:30 • It is 30 minutes from 8:30 to 9:00 and 15 minutes from 9:00 to 9:15. 30 + 15 = 45 minutes	*Level 3 Number* *This question is testing calculation with time, and understanding a timetable.* See *Collins KS3 Maths Total Revision*, page 4
(b)	1	09.30	• To reach Colton by 10:30 you have to work back to find the latest bus that arrives before 10:30. This is the bus that arrives at 10:15, which leaves at 9:30.	
(c)	1	£11	• You can write the answer in several ways e.g. £11.00, 1100p (but you must leave out the £ sign), £11-00, £11,00, 11 pounds 00. You could also write £11.00p or £11 00 pence but these last two are not strictly correct so you should avoid writing answers like that. • Answers that are not acceptable are £1100p or £11.0. You must not mix units incorrectly and you must not use decimal points incorrectly. Money answers in pounds should always have two decimal places.	*This question is testing basic number work and an understanding of money.* See *Collins KS3 Maths Total Revision*, pages 2 and 4
Total	**4**			

Question 2

Part	Mark	Answer	Tutorial	What's this question looking for?
(a)	1		• You can use tracing paper if you prefer, or you can measure the angles with a protractor. If you do measure them the answers are 55°, 25°, 55°, 140° and 88°. • The question asks you to circle the answers. Any clear indication is acceptable: for example you would still get the full marks if you ticked the correct angles, or you could write down the values.	*Level 3 Shape, space and measures* *This question is testing basic angle work.* See Collins KS3 Maths Total Revision, page 83
(b)	1	Any angle bigger than 90° is correct. The following are all good answers.	• Notice that (a) is not marked with an angle. There is no problem as both possible answers are correct. • The angle in (c) is a straight line. The angle must be marked. • In (d) the angle is a reflex angle bigger than 270°. This must be marked, as the answer could be taken as the acute angle and this would be wrong.	
(c)	1	South	• This is fairly straightforward – if you know which direction clockwise is. In the past, all clocks had hands which moved round. Now many clocks are digital so it is not as easy to remember. You just have to learn the directions – or buy an old-fashioned watch!	
(d)	1	South	• Just be careful that you start off facing west and turn clockwise.	
Total	**4**			

Question 3

Part	Mark	Answer	Tutorial	What's this question looking for?
(a)	1	20 miles	• The table shows the distances from Shrewsbury, so the answer to this problem is the number in the table.	*Level 3 Number* *This question is testing basic number work and use of tables.* See Collins KS3 Maths Total Revision, page 1

Part	Mark	Answer	Tutorial	What's this question looking for?
(b)	1	53 miles	• To find this answer you have to look up the distance from Shrewsbury to Borth and then subtract the answer from part (a). 73 – 20 = 53	
(c)	1	9 miles	• This is worked out as 82 – 73 = 9. • Note that if you don't write down the units in at least one part of the question you will lose the third mark.	
Total	3			

Question 4

Part	Mark	Answer	Tutorial	What's this question looking for?
	1		• You can use tracing paper or a mirror to help you. The lines of symmetry must be long enough to go from the edge to a point past the centre. It is a good idea to draw them as long as possible. • If you have more lines than shown in the answers you will not get any marks. A common mistake is to have only two lines in the second drawing.	*Level 3 Shape, space and measures* *This question is testing understanding of line symmetry.* See *Collins KS3 Maths Total Revision*. page 33
	1			
	1			
Total	3			

THIS IS THE START OF THE TIER 4–6 PAPER

Question 5

Part	Mark	Answer	Tutorial	What's this question looking for?
(a)	1 1 1	10 16 30	• This question is about calculating volume by counting cubes. There are other ways of working out the volume of cuboids. One way is to multiply the width by the depth by the height. It doesn't matter which way you do it as long as you do one or the other.	*Level 3–4 Shape, space and measures* *This question involves working out volumes by counting cubes.* **See Collins KS3 Maths Total Revision, page 36**
(b)	1	24	• This is also about volume. There are two different parts to this shape. It is best to think of it as two different cuboids split like this: **Note:** The Tier 4–6 Paper starts with the third cuboid in part (a) of question 5 and also includes part (b). Therefore the total mark for this question in Tiers 4–6 is 2.	
Total	**4**			

Question 6

Part	Mark	Answer	Tutorial	What's this question looking for?
(a)	1 1	Any pair of numbers that add up to 34 (e.g. 24 and 10 or 30 and 4). Any pair of numbers that multiply together to give 10 (e.g. 1 and 10 or 2 and 5).	• There is no reason why you could not use decimals or fractions. However they are not the simplest answers. Use whole numbers as these are easier to deal with.	*Level 3–4 Number* *This question is testing basic number work.* **See Collins KS3 Maths Total Revision, page 1**
(b)	1	12	• This answer is found from basic tables.	**Note:** Parts (a) and (b) of question 6 are not in the Tier 4–6 Paper. Therefore the total mark for this question in Tiers 4–6 is 4.

Part	Mark	Answer	Tutorial	What's this question looking for?
(c)	1	275	• This is a subtraction. You should set it up like this: $\begin{array}{r} 5^{4}\ 12^{1}\ 1^{1}4 \\ -\ 2\ \ \ 4\ \ \ 9 \\ \hline 2\ \ \ 7\ \ \ 5 \end{array}$ The carried figures are not necessary but they may help you with your working. • Another way to do this problem is to count on, as you may have done with the 'time' problem above. e.g. (number line) 200 250 300 350 400 450 500 550 600 51 + 100 + 100 + 24 = 275	
	1	368	• This is short multiplication. You should set it up like this: $\begin{array}{r} 4\ \ 6 \\ \times\ \ \ \ \ \ 8 \\ \hline 3\ \ 6^{4}\ \ 8 \end{array}$ • The carried figures are not necessary but they may help you with your working. • Another way to do this problem is to work out $8 \times 40 = 320$ and $8 \times 6 = 48$ then add the answers. $320 + 48 = 368$	
	1	16	• This is short division. You should set the sum up like this: $\begin{array}{r} 1\ \ 6\ \ \ \ \\ 9\overline{)1\ \ 4\ \ ^{5}4} \end{array}$ • The carried figures are not necessary but they may help you with your working. • Another way to do this problem is: $10 \times 16 = 160$ $160 - 16 = 144$ • There is no remainder but if you wrote the answer as 16 remainder 0 you would not lose any marks.	
Total	6			

Question 7

Part	Mark	Answer	Tutorial	What's this question looking for?
(a)	1	£40	• This is almost long multiplication but because it involves the 25 times table it is only level 4. The 25 times table is regarded as straightforward as it can be connected with money. • Every 4 'lots' of 25 give 100, so every 4 'lots' of £2.50 make £10. • 16 is 4 'lots' of 4 so the cost of 16 video tapes is 4 'lots' of £10 which is £40.	*Level 4 Number* *This question is testing basic number work and understanding of money.* See *Collins KS3 Maths Total Revision*, pages 1 and 57
(b)	1	£5.96	• This is short multiplication even though it involves decimals. Prices such as £1.49 and £2.99 are common in shops. This work is still level 4 because if you add 1 penny the price is £1.50 per cassette. So the price of 4 cassettes is 4 × £1.50 = £6.00. From this you have to take away 4p so the answer is £5.96. • If you do it as a short multiplication sum it should be set out like this: $$\begin{array}{r} 1\ \ 4\ \ 9 \\ \times \qquad 4 \\ \hline 5^1\ \ 9^3\ \ 6 \end{array}$$	
(c)	1	8 cassettes	• Basically you have to divide £12 by £1.49. This is far too difficult for level 4 but if you work out the number of £1.50s in £12 the problem is much easier. The £1.50 'times table' is £1.50, £3.00, £4.50, £6.00 and so on. It is easy to work out that 8 × £1.50 = £12.00.	
(d)	1	3 packs	• This is worked out as 'How many £4.00s are there in £12.00?' $12 \div 4 = 3$ The real sum is $12 \div 3.99$ which, as you can easily see, is 3 packs with 3p left over.	
(e)	1	11 cassettes (3 packs of 3 cassettes and 2 single cassettes)	• You already know that you can buy 3 packs with £12. This leaves £3.03. Two single cassettes cost $2 \times £1.50 - 2p = £2.98$. You can give this answer as 3 packs and 2 cassettes or you could give the total cost of the 11 cassettes (£14.95). This is not the best way to answer the question but the only way you would have found the answer of £14.95 is if you worked it out properly.	
Total	5			

Question 8

Part	Mark	Answer	Tutorial	What's this question looking for?
	1 1 1 1	63 21 40 8	● The question explains what a magic square is. The first thing to do is add up the numbers in the top row (which is given) to get 63. This is then used to work out the missing numbers because two of the numbers in each row, column or diagonal are given. The full square is: $$\begin{array}{|c|c|c|} \hline 24 & 34 & 5 \\ \hline 2 & 21 & 40 \\ \hline 37 & 8 & 18 \\ \hline \end{array}$$ ● Because it is easy to be careless adding up the numbers, follow-through is allowed on these answers. For example, if you found 53 as your total, then you would have this square: $$\begin{array}{|c|c|c|} \hline 24 & 34 & 5 \\ \hline 2 & 11 & 30 \\ \hline 37 & -2 & 18 \\ \hline \end{array}$$ The centre cell is correct if it is **your total** minus 42. The centre right cell is correct if it is **your total** minus 23. The bottom centre cell is correct if it is **your total** minus 55.	*Level 4 Number* *This question is testing basic number work.* See *Collins KS3 Maths Total Revision*, page 1
Total	4			

Question 9

Part	Mark	Answer	Tutorial	What's this question looking for?
(a)	1	1000, 1500 and 1250	● The first mark is for giving the correct values, in grams, for each ingredient. These are 1000, 1500 and 1250. You can use a comma to separate the thousands digit, if this is what you usually do.	*Level 4 Shape, space and measures* *This question involves metric units and conversion between them.* See *Collins KS3 Maths Total Revision*, page 35
	2	1, 1.5, 1.25	● The second two marks are for converting the values in grams to values in kilograms. The last two can be written as $1\frac{1}{2}$ and $1\frac{1}{4}$, or the three could be written as 1.000, 1.500 and 1.250. You need to know that there are 1000 grams in a kilogram and that dividing by 1000 means 'moving the decimal point' back three places.	
(b)	1	£3.50	● This is really a number problem. You need to realise that there are 5 'lots' of 6 in 30. This means you need 5 'lots' of 70p. $5 \times 70 = 350$. This can be written as 350p or as £3.50. You will remember from question 1(c) that there are several ways of writing down money answers.	
Total	4			

THIS IS THE START OF THE TIER 5–7 PAPER

Question 10

Part	Mark	Answer	Tutorial	What's this question looking for?
(a)	1	4 corner pieces, 12 edge pieces, 8 middle pieces	• You can count pieces of each type.	*Level 4–5 Number* *This question is testing recognition of number patterns and square numbers.*
(b)	2	4 corner pieces, 18 edge pieces, 20 middle pieces	• You cannot count the missing pieces without some sort of drawing. You might split up the jigsaw like this: or like this: ```
1   5   1
1 ┌─────────┐ 1
│   │
4 │   │ 4
│   │
1 └─────────┘ 1
1   5   1
```   ```
C E E E E C
C M M M M M C
C M M M M M C
C M M M M M C
C M M M M M C
C E E E E C
`` • You can gain 1 mark if you get two of the three numbers right, or get the right numbers in the wrong order.	See *Collins KS3 Maths Total Revision*, pages 19 and 21 **Note:** Part (b) of question 10 is not in the Tier 5–7 Paper. Therefore the total mark for this question in Tiers 5–7 is 3.
| **(c)** | 2 | 4 corner pieces, 32 edge pieces, 100 pieces in total | • You have to realise that the middle pieces form a square 8 pieces by 8 pieces.<br>There are always four corner pieces.<br>There will be 4 lots of 8 edge pieces.<br><br>```
 1    8   1
1 ┌───────┐ 1
  │       │
8 │  64   │ 8
  │       │
 1 └───────┘ 1
 1    8   1
```<br><br>• The total is 100 because there are 10 pieces on each edge.<br>**Note:** There is a clue in the question. The last value must be a square number because it says so. | |
| **Total** | **5** | | | |
```

Question 11

Part	Mark	Answer	Tutorial	What's this question looking for?
(a)	2	For full marks you have to show something like: 10% of 240 = 24 5% of 240 = 12 $2\frac{1}{2}$% of 240 = 6 so $17\frac{1}{2}$% of 240 = 42	• There are many other ways of finding $17\frac{1}{2}$%. For example you can find 10%, 7% and $\frac{1}{2}$%. To gain the first mark, the percentages you write down must add up to $17\frac{1}{2}$%. To gain the second mark your answer must be 42. The method shown on the left is the easiest to work out. Other ways of doing the problem are: • find 2 lots of 10% then take away $2\frac{1}{2}$% • work out 20%, 10%, 5%. Add them up to get 35% and then halve the answer.	*Level 5 Number* *This question involves simple percentages.* See *Collins KS3 Maths Total Revision*, page 64
(b)	2	For full marks you have to show something like: 10% of 520 = 52 20% of 520 = 104 5% of 520 = 26 35% of 520 = 182	• Again there are several ways of doing this. You can find 10%, 10%, 10% and 5% for example. To gain the first mark you must list percentages that add up to 35% and show that you have attempted to add up the percentages or the answers. To gain the second mark you have to get the answer of 182. You could also work out $35 \div 100 \times 520$ or 0.35×520, or find $17\frac{1}{2}$% as you did in part (a) and then double the answer.	
Total	**4**			

Question 12

Part	Mark	Answer	Tutorial	What's this question looking for?
(a)	1	14 packs	• This is long division. There are a couple of ways of doing long division. The first is the traditional method: $\begin{array}{r} 1\ \ 3\ \ \text{r}\,12 \\ 16\overline{)2\ \ 2\ \ 0} \\ \underline{1\ \ 6} \\ 6\ \ 0 \\ \underline{4\ \ 8} \\ \underline{1\ \ 2} \end{array}$ • As the remainder is fairly easy to work out you may have done this like a short division. $\begin{array}{r} 1\ \ 3\ \ \text{r}\,12 \\ 16\overline{)2\ \ 2\ \ {}^{6}0} \end{array}$ • Another method is the method of repeated subtraction: $\begin{array}{rr} & 220 \\ 10 \times 16 = & \underline{160} \\ & 60 \\ 2 \times 16 = & \underline{32} \\ & 28 \\ 1 \times 16 = & \underline{16} \\ & \underline{12} \end{array}$	*Level 5 Number* *This question involves long division.* See *Collins KS3 Maths Total Revision*, page 55

Part	Mark	Answer	Tutorial	What's this question looking for?
	1		• The number of 16s in 220 is 13 remainder 12, which means that the teacher will need 14 packs. • An answer of 14 gains 2 marks. If you make one mistake, or say 13 packs, you will only gain 1 mark.	
(b)	2 1	10 560 g 10.56 kg	• This is long multiplication. • There are several ways of doing this. Four methods are shown in *Collins KS3 Mathematics Study & Revision Guide*. One of them is Chinese multiplication or Napier's bones, which would look like this: Note the carry digits. • An answer of 10 560 gains 2 marks. If you make one mistake you can still gain 1 mark. • To gain the last mark you need to convert your answer from grams to kilograms. This means dividing by 1000. You can still gain this mark from your answer even if it is wrong. Your answer must be over 1000 and not a multiple of 1000. You can also give a rounded or truncated answer, so 10.5 kg or 11 kg is acceptable, but it is not a good idea to round unless you are asked to do so.	*This part of the question involves long multiplication.* See *Collins KS3 Maths Total Revision*, page 53
Total	**5**			

Question 13

Part	Mark	Answer	Tutorial	What's this question looking for?
(a)	1	$n + 5$	• There are lots of rules about what you can and cannot do with algebra. Another acceptable answer is $5 + n$ or $N + 5$ or $5 + N$, but $x + 5$ is wrong. You cannot change letters. Neither can you simplify expressions wrongly. So $n + 5 = 5n$ would be wrong but $m = n + 5$ would be allowed as it could be read as 'number of marbles $= n + 5$'. It is safer to write down the expression without using equals signs and not to try to simplify the answer unless the questions says 'write your answer as simply as possible' or 'simplify your answer'.	*Level 5 Algebra* *This question involves simple formulae.* See *Collins KS3 Maths Total Revision*, page 75

Part	Mark	Answer	Tutorial	What's this question looking for?
(b)	1	$t - 2$	• In this case $2 - t$ is wrong. You can change additions such as $n + 5$ and $5 + n$ around but you cannot change subtractions around. One way to check if your answer is right is to try out a number example. If Ravi had 9 marbles he would end up with $9 - 2 = 7$, but $2 - 9$ is ⁻7.	
(c)	2	You should have these boxes ticked: ☐ ✓ ☐ ✓ ✓ ☐	• The expressions for each line are First line: $p - 2 + p + p = 3p - 2$ Second line: $p - 2 + p - 2 + p - 2 = 3p - 6$ Third line: $p - 3 + p + p = 3p - 3$ Fourth line: $p - 3 + p - 3 + p = 3p - 6$ Fifth line: $p - 6 + p + p = 3p - 6$ Sixth line: $p - 6 + p - 6 + p = 3p - 12$ • Each of these includes $3p$ because that is what you started with. The rest of the expression is the number of marbles taken out altogether. If you miss a box or tick a wrong box you can still gain 1 mark.	
Total	**4**			

Question 14

Part	Mark	Answer	Tutorial	What's this question looking for?
(a)	2	Q, R and T in any order.	• Each bar in the graphs is a multiple of 10%. So in graph P, 10% scored 4, 5 and 6, 30% scored 7 and 20% scored 8 and 9. Basically, you have to add up the totals reached by the bars on the side axis. You can see easily that graphs Q, R and T are the correct ones.	*Level 5 Handling data* *This question involves bar charts and means.* **See *Collins KS3 Maths Total Revision*, page 41**
(b)	2	You should have these boxes ticked: ☐ ✓ ☐ ✓	• The statements only have to be true for graphs Q, R and T. • Statement 1 is false because in class Q and class T pupils scored less than 2. • Statement 2 is true because you already know that 80% scored over 7 for these graphs. 80% is most of the class. • Statement 3 is false because only pupils in class T scored 10 or more. Only 10% did. 10% is not most of the class. • Statement 4 is true because some pupils in all the classes scored less than 6. • If you get one wrong, or tick an incorrect box, you can still gain 1 mark. You can also gain both marks if you make a mistake in part (a) but follow it through correctly.	

Part	Mark	Answer	Tutorial	What's this question looking for?
(c)	1	You can shade any boxes that make the mean 6.	• As 80% scored 6 and 10% have scored 5 this means that whatever is shaded must be equivalent to 10% scoring 7. The easiest way to do this is to shade in like this: • Another answer might be: 	
Total	5			

THIS IS THE END OF THE TIER 3–5 PAPER

> ## THIS IS THE START OF THE TIER 6–8 PAPER

Question 15

Part	Mark	Answer	Tutorial	What's this question looking for?
	3	Graph 1 – C, Graph 2 – A, Graph 3 – E	• Graph 1 shows that the depth of the water increases quickly at first, then at a slower rate. This means that the container must be getting wider as it fills up, so it is container C. • Graph 2 shows that the depth of the water increases at a constant rate. This means that the container must stay the same width as it fills up, so it is container A. • Graph 3 shows that the depth of the water increases fairly quickly at first, then slows down when the container is about half full. Then it increases at a faster rate. This means that the container must be getting wider at first and then becomes narrower as it fills up, so it is container E. • You would gain 1 mark for each correct answer.	*Level 6 Algebra* *This question is testing the interpretation of graphs that describe real-life situations.* See *Collins KS3 Maths Total Revision*, page 231 question 11
Total	3			

Question 16

Part	Mark	Answer	Tutorial	What's this question looking for?
(a)	1	$x = 8$	• Lines that are drawn horizontally, parallel to the x-axis, are of the form $y = a$, where a is the value where the line crosses the y-axis. • Lines that are drawn vertically, parallel to the y-axis, are of the form $x = b$, where b is the value where the line crosses the x-axis. • The line through A and B passes through the point 8 on the x-axis and so has the equation $x = 8$. You would gain no marks if you wrote 'x is 8'.	*Level 6 Algebra* *This question is testing ability to draw linear graphs.* See *Collins KS3 Maths Total Revision*, page 132
(b)	1	$y = x + 7$ or $x = y - 7$ or $y - x = 7$	• Lines that go diagonally across a graph are of the form $y = mx + c$, where m is the gradient of the line and c is where the line crosses the y-axis. • The line through F and E is parallel to the line through A and D and therefore has the same gradient with $m = 1$. The line passes through the point 7 on the y-axis, so $c = 7$. The equation of the line is $y = 1x + 7$ which is better written as $y = x + 7$.	

Part	Mark	Answer	Tutorial	What's this question looking for?
(c)	1	$y = x - 1$ or $x = y + 1$ or $x - y = 1$	• The line through B and C is parallel to the other two lines, so again $m = 1$. If you extend the line it will pass through the point $^-1$ on the y-axis, so $c = {}^-1$. The equation of the line is therefore $y = x - 1$.	
Total	**3**			

Question 17

Part	Mark	Answer	Tutorial	What's this question looking for?
(a)	1	2.5 or $2\frac{1}{2}$	• The formulae for the area of 2-D shapes that you need to know are given at the front of the test papers. The formula for the area of a parallelogram is $A = bh$. If $A = 10$ and $b = 4$, then $10 = 4h$ and so $h = \frac{10}{4} = 2\frac{1}{2}$.	*Level 6 Shape, space and measures* *This question involves finding the area of 2-D shapes.* **See *Collins KS3 Maths Total Revision*, page 148**
(b)	1	10	• The formula for the area of a triangle is $A = \frac{1}{2}bh$. If $A = 10$ and $h = 2$, then $10 = \frac{1}{2} \times b \times 2$ and so $b = 10$.	
(c)	1 1	Any value of h from the table, with corresponding values of a and b, so that $(a + b) \times h = 20$ and $a > b$. Different values for h, a and b, from the table, with $a > b$. <table><tr><th>h</th><th>$a + b$</th></tr><tr><td>1</td><td>20</td></tr><tr><td>2</td><td>10</td></tr><tr><td>2.5</td><td>8</td></tr><tr><td>$3\frac{1}{3}$</td><td>6</td></tr><tr><td>4</td><td>5</td></tr><tr><td>5</td><td>4</td></tr><tr><td>10</td><td>2</td></tr><tr><td>20</td><td>1</td></tr></table>	• The formula for the area of a trapezium is $A = \frac{1}{2}(a + b) \times h$. If $A = 10$, then $(a + b) \times h = 20$. So you first need to find two numbers which when multiplied together give 20, such as 4 and 5. This would give $a + b = 4$ and $h = 5$, but since $a > b$, $a = 3$ and $b = 1$ are possible answers. The table shows all the different combinations for $a + b$ and h that you are likely to choose. You can have the same value for h in both parts of the question, but you must have different values for a and b.	

Part	Mark	Answer	Tutorial	What's this question looking for?
(d)	2	length = 4 cm, width = 2.5 cm	• Find x first by noticing that the two expressions for the length of the rectangle must be equal. This gives the equation: $10x - 1 = 4x + 2$ (Take $4x$ from both sides) $6x - 1 = 2$ (Add 1 to both sides) $6x = 3$ (Divide both sides by 6) $x = 0.5$ • The length of the rectangle is $4x + 2 = 4$ or $10x - 1 = 4$. The formula for the area of a rectangle is $A = lw$. If $A = 10$ and $l = 4$, then $10 = 4w$. This gives $w = \frac{10}{4} = 2.5$. You would gain 1 mark if you showed that $x = 0.5$ or that $l = 4$.	Note: Part (d) of question 17 does not appear on the Tier 4–6 Paper. Therefore the total mark for this question in Tiers 4–6 is 4.
Total	6			

Question 18

Part	Mark	Answer	Tutorial	What's this question looking for?
(a)	2	<table><tr><td>5</td><td>6</td><td>10</td></tr><tr><td>16</td><td>17</td><td>32</td></tr></table>	• From the three patterns given, notice that the number of grey tiles is always 1 more than the pattern number, and the number of white tiles is always double the pattern number. • You would gain 1 mark if you gave two or three correct values or if you got the colours the wrong way round.	*Level 6 Algebra* *This question is testing ability to find the rule for the nth term of a sequence.* See *Collins KS3 Maths Total Revision*, page 121
(b)	2	<table><tr><td></td><td>grey</td><td>white</td></tr><tr><td>n</td><td>$n + 1$</td><td>$2n$</td></tr></table>	• The question asks for expressions for the number of grey and white tiles, so you must use n in your answers, as shown in the table. Do not use equations such as $n = n + 1$, as you would lose marks. You could write 'number of tiles $= n + 1$', but try to avoid using equations when questions ask you to write expressions. For $2n$ you could also write $2 \times n$ or $n + n$.	
(c)	1	$3n + 1$	• The total number of tiles in pattern number n is $n + 1 + 2n$ which simplifies to $3n + 1$. When simplifying expressions, collect the 'like terms' together first, then the numbers.	
(d)	2	$5n + 4$	• The number of grey tiles in the pattern follows the sequence 4, 6, 8 … increasing by 2 each time. The number of grey tiles in pattern number n is therefore $2n + 2$. The number of white tiles in the pattern follows the sequence 5, 8, 11 … increasing by 3 each time. The number of white tiles in pattern n is therefore $3n + 2$. So the total number of tiles in pattern n is $2n + 2 + 3n + 2$ which simplifies to $5n + 4$.	Note: Part (d) of question 18 does not appear on the Tier 4–6 Paper. Therefore the total mark for this question in Tiers 4–6 is 5.
Total	7			

Question 19

Part	Mark	Answer	Tutorial	What's this question looking for?
(a)	1	250	• If $2.4 \times 25 = 60$, then $0.24 \times 250 = 60$. Notice that to find two multiplications that have the same answer, if you divide one of the numbers by an amount (10 here), then the other number must be multiplied by the same amount. • You can, of course, do a division sum without a calculator: $$\frac{60}{0.24} = \frac{600}{2.4} = \frac{6000}{24} = 250$$	*Level 6 Algebra* *This question is testing ability to solve equations by algebraic methods.* See *Collins KS3 Maths Total Revision*, pages 124 and 184
	1	0.1 or $\frac{1}{10}$	• If $60 \div 1 = 60$, then $6 \div 0.1 = 60$. Notice that to find divisions that have the same answer, if you divide one of the numbers by an amount (10 here), then the other number must also be divided by the same amount.	
(b)	1	$a = 20$	• $5a - 40 = 60$ (Add 40 to both sides) $5a = 100$ (Divide both sides by 5) $a = 20$	
	1	$b = ^-5$	• $4b + 80 = 60$ (Take away 80 from both sides) $4b = ^-20$ (Divide both sides by 4) $b = ^-5$	
	1	$c = 6$ or $c = ^-6$, or both	• $c^2 + 24 = 60$ (Take away 24 from both sides) $c^2 = 36$ (Take the square root of both sides) $c = 6$ Since $\sqrt{36}$ is also $^-6$, this answer would also be accepted.	The total mark for question 19 in Tiers 4–6 is 5.
Total	**5**			

THIS IS THE END OF THE TIER 4–6 PAPER

Question 19 (continued)

Part	Mark	Answer	Tutorial	What's this question looking for?

(c)	3	$x = 20$ and $y = 5$	• Write down the two simultaneous equations:
			$x + 8y = 60$ (1)
			$4x - 4y = 60$ (2)
			Balance the two equations to make the xs or the ys the same. For example:
			(1) × 1 and (2) × 2 makes the ys the same.
			$x + 8y = 60$ (3)
			$8x - 8y = 120$ (4)
			Now add (3) and (4) to eliminate y.
			    $9x = 180$ (Divide both sides by 9)
			      $x = 20$ (Substitute this into equation (1))
			$20 + 8y = 60$ (Take away 20 from both sides)
			    $8y = 40$ (Divide both sides by 8)
			     $y = 5$ (Check in equation (2))
			$80 - 20 = 60$ which is correct
			• You would gain 2 marks if you gave the correct value for x or y, and 1 mark if you showed some of the above working, but made careless errors.
				The total mark for question 19 in Tiers 5–7 and 6–8 is 8.

Total	**8**			

Question 20

Part	Mark	Answer	Tutorial	What's this question looking for?
	2	The completed diagram should look like this: 	• The line on the diagram that shows the position of the fence must be drawn 2 squares from the edge of the lawn. This line can be drawn in three parts. i) The line which is 2 squares from the circular part of the lawn is found by drawing a semi-circle with a radius of 6 squares to give: ii) The line which is 2 squares from the base of the lawn is found by drawing a straight line 8 squares long to give: 	*Level 7 Shape, space and measures* *This question is testing ability to draw the locus of a point.* See *Collins KS3 Maths Total Revision*, page 202

77

Part	Mark	Answer	Tutorial	What's this question looking for?
			iii) The lines that are 2 squares from the corners of the lawn are found by drawing two circular arcs with a radius of 2 squares to give: • Some allowance is for diagrams that are slightly inaccurate, but try to avoid drawing lines freehand. You are expected to show that you can use a ruler and a pair of compasses in the tests. • You would gain 1 mark for an otherwise correct diagram with the two circular arcs wrongly drawn or omitted.	
Total	**2**			

Question 21

Part	Mark	Answer	Tutorial	What's this question looking for?
	2	Any correct method to show that the statement is wrong.	• The easiest way to show that the statement is wrong is by substituting numbers for t and w into both sides of the equation and then showing that the answers obtained are not the same. For example, let $t = 2$ and $w = 4$. Then the left-hand side becomes $\frac{1}{2} + \frac{1}{4} = \frac{2}{4} + \frac{1}{4} = \frac{3}{4}$ and the right–hand side becomes $\frac{2}{6} = \frac{1}{3}$. $\frac{3}{4}$ is not equal to $\frac{1}{3}$. So the answers on both sides are not equal, and we have found an example to prove the pupil is wrong. • You could also let t and w have the same value, which may be slightly easier. For example, let $t = 2$ and $w = 2$. Then the left-hand side becomes $\frac{1}{2} + \frac{1}{2} = 1$ and the right-hand side becomes $\frac{2}{4} = \frac{1}{2}$. 1 is not equal to $\frac{1}{2}$. So the answers on both sides are not equal, and we have found another example to prove the pupil is wrong. • You could also use algebra as shown below but this is probably more difficult, as it is level 8 work. $\frac{1}{t} + \frac{1}{w} = \frac{w + t}{tw}$ which is not the same as $\frac{2}{t + w}$.	*Level 7 Number* *This question is testing the manipulation of fractions.*
Total	**2**			

Question 22

Part	Mark	Answer	Tutorial	What's this question looking for?
(a)	1	$\frac{80}{100}$ or $\frac{4}{5}$ or 0.8	• The number of customers waiting 2 minutes or longer is found by adding the last three frequencies of the bar chart: $40 + 30 + 10 = 80$. So P(customer waits for 2 minutes or longer) $= \frac{80}{100} = \frac{4}{5}$. • Probability is written as a fraction or a decimal. Always cancel fractions if it is possible, although you would not lose marks if you did not. You would get no marks, though, for writing '80 out of 100' or '80 in 100'.	*Level 7 Handling data* *This question is testing estimation of the mean from a grouped frequency diagram.* See *Collins KS3 Maths Total Revision*, page 216
(b)	1	$\frac{60}{100}$ or $\frac{3}{5}$ or 0.6	• There were 40 customers waiting from 2 to 3 minutes, so approximately 20 customers were waiting between 2.5 and 3 minutes. Therefore the number of customers waiting 2.5 minutes or longer is $20 + 30 + 10 = 60$. So P(customer waits for 2.5 minutes or longer) $= \frac{60}{100} = \frac{3}{5}$.	
(c)	2	2.74	• The last column of the table is given below: $\begin{array}{r} fx \\ \hline 3 \\ 21 \\ 100 \\ 105 \\ \underline{45} \\ \mathbf{274} \end{array}$ The mean $= \dfrac{\text{total waiting time for all customers}}{\text{total number of customers}}$ $= \dfrac{274}{100}$ $= 2.74$. • You would gain 1 mark if your total in the fx column was wrong but you correctly divided this by 100.	
(d)	1	Possible answers are: do it for a longer time, or do more checkouts, or decrease the time intervals, or do it on different days.	• Make sure that you read the question carefully. You are already told one way of improving the survey, so you need to give a different way. Do not give answers that are irrelevant, such as 'draw a pie chart' or 'use the mode'.	
Total	**5**			

Question 23

Part	Mark	Answer	Tutorial	What's this question looking for?
(a)	1	1500	• When $p = 10$, $a = \frac{3}{2} \times 10^3 = \frac{3}{2} \times 10 \times 10 \times 10 = \frac{3000}{2} = 1500$	*Level 7 Algebra* *This question is testing skills in manipulation of algebraic expressions.*
	1	20	• When $p = 10$, $b = \dfrac{2 \times 10^2 \times (10 - 3)}{7 \times 10} = \dfrac{2 \times 100 \times 7}{70} = \dfrac{1400}{70}$ $= 20$	See *Collins KS3 Maths Total Revision,* page 230 question 9
(b)	1	$\dfrac{3d}{5}$	• $\dfrac{3cd^2}{5cd} = \dfrac{3 \times \cancel{c} \times \cancel{d} \times d}{5 \times \cancel{c} \times \cancel{d}} = \dfrac{3 \times d}{5} = \dfrac{3d}{5}$ Notice how the c and d cancel out.	The total mark for question 23 in Tiers 5–7 is 3.
Total	**3**			

THIS IS THE END OF THE TIER 5–7 PAPER

Question 23 (continued)

Part	Mark	Answer	Tutorial	What's this question looking for?
(c)	1	$9x - 14$	• This question involves expanding brackets, so you need to know that: $a(b + c) = ab + ac$ and $-a(b + c) = -ab - ac$ $3(x - 2) - 2(4 - 3x) = 3x - 6 - 8 + 6x = 9x - 14$ Notice the change in sign when expanding the second bracket.	
	1	$x^2 + 5x + 6$	• The next three parts involve expanding two brackets, so you need to know that: $(a + b)(c + d) = a(c + d) + b(c + d)$ $\qquad\qquad\qquad = ac + ad + bc + bd$ $(x + 2)(x + 3) = x^2 + 3x + 2x + 6$ $\qquad\qquad\qquad = x^2 + 5x + 6$	
	1	$x^2 + 3x - 4$	• $(x + 4)(x - 1) = x^2 - x + 4x - 4$ $\qquad\qquad\qquad = x^2 + 3x - 4$	
	1	$x^2 - 4x + 4$	• $(x - 2)^2 = (x - 2)(x - 2)$ $\qquad\quad = x^2 - 2x - 2x + 4$ $\qquad\quad = x^2 - 4x + 4$	The total mark for question 23 in Tiers 6–8 is 7.
Total	**7**			

Question 24

Part	Mark	Answer	Tutorial	What's this question looking for?
(a)	1	Your graph should look like this:	• $2x^2 = 2 \times x^2$, so for each value of x^2, the y-value is twice as large as in $y = x^2$. This will make the curve steeper, but notice the curve still passes through the origin.	*Level 8 Algebra* *This question is testing the interpretation of quadratic graphs.*
(b)	1	$y = -x^2$	• Curve A is a reflection of $y = x^2$ in the x-axis, so all the y-values will now become negative.	
(c)	1	$y = x^2 + 1$	• The translation will add 1 to all the y-values, so the equation of curve B is $y = x^2 + 1$.	
(d)	2	$y < 2$ and $y > x^2$	• The shaded region is below the line $y = 2$, so $y < 2$ is one inequality that describes the region. The shaded region is also above the curve $y = x^2$, so $y > x^2$ is the other inequality that describes the region. • You will gain 1 mark for each correct inequality. You would get no marks if you ringed $y < 2$ and $y > 2$ or $y < x^2$ and $y > x^2$, as these are conflicting inequalities.	
Total	**5**			

Question 25

Part	Mark	Answer	Tutorial	What's this question looking for?
(a)	1	4×10^3 is a larger number than 4^3 $4 \times 10^3 = 4000$ and $4^3 = 64$	• This part is about using numbers written in standard form. 4×10^3 is a shorter way of writing 4×1000 or 4000. • For example 4 000 000 can be written as $4 \times 1 000 000$ or, in standard form, as 4×10^6.	*Level 8 Number* *This question is testing the use of numbers expressed in standard form.* See *Collins KS3 Maths Total Revision,* page 227 question 1
(b)	1	0.36×10^5	• $3.6 \times 10^4 = 3.6 \times 10\ 000 = 36\ 000$. This is the same as 0.36×10^5 or $0.36 \times 100\ 000$.	

Part	Mark	Answer	Tutorial	What's this question looking for?
(c)	1	25×10^{-4}	• This part is about negative indices and the table below shows you how to use them. | Number	Index form
---	---
1000	10^3
100	10^2
10	10^1
1	10^0
0.1	10^{-1}
0.01	10^{-2}
0.001	10^{-3}	 $2.5 \times 10^{-3} = 2.5 \times 0.001 = 0.0025$. This is the same as 25×10^{-4} or 25×0.0001.	
(d)	1	6 or 6×10^0	• This part uses the fact that $10^a \times 10^b = 10^{a+b}$ $(3 \times 10^2) \times (2 \times 10^{-2}) = 6 \times 10^{2-2} = 6 \times 10^0 = 6$.	
	1	30 000 or 3×10^4	• This part uses the fact that $\frac{10^a}{10^b} = 10^{a-b}$ $\frac{6 \times 10^8}{2 \times 10^4} = 3 \times 10^4$ or 30 000	
Total	5			

Question 26

Part	Mark	Answer	Tutorial	What's this question looking for?
(a)	1	$\frac{69}{100}$ or 0.69	• 39 students study only French and 30 students study only German, so 69 study only one of the languages. Therefore P(a student studies only one of the languages) $= \frac{69}{100}$.	*Level 8 Handling data* *This question is testing calculation of the probabilities of compound events.* See *Collins KS3 Maths Total Revision*, page 234 question 16
(b)	1	$\frac{27}{57}$ or 0.47	• There are 57 students who study German and 27 of them also study French. Therefore P(a student who studies German also studies French) $= \frac{27}{57}$. This can be given as a decimal, but the answer must round to 0.47.	

Part	Mark	Answer	Tutorial	What's this question looking for?
(c)	1	$\frac{27}{100} \times \frac{26}{99}$	• For this question you need to know that for two events A and B: P(A and B) = P(A) × P(B) provided A and B are independent events (i.e. an outcome from one event does not determine an outcome of the other event). P(first student studies French and German) $= \frac{27}{100}$ • If another student is chosen this leaves 99 students to chose from, of whom 26 now study French and German. So P(second student studies French and German) $= \frac{26}{99}$ P(both students study French and German) $= \frac{27}{100} \times \frac{26}{99}$	
Total	**3**			

Question 27

Part	Mark	Answer	Tutorial	What's this question looking for?
(a)	3	$\frac{9\pi a^2}{2} + \frac{4\pi a^2}{2} - \frac{\pi a^2}{2}$ $= 6\pi a^2$	• This is an example of an unstructured question. This means that you have to do more than one step to get the answer. It usually involves showing a fair amount of working. The formula for the area of a circle is $A = \pi r^2$, so the formula for the area of a semi-circle is $A = \frac{1}{2}\pi r^2$. Now use this formula to calculate the area of each separate semi-circle. For the large semi-circle $r = 3a$. So $A = \frac{\pi r^2}{2} = \frac{\pi \times (3a)^2}{2} = \frac{\pi \times 3a \times 3a}{2} = \frac{9\pi a^2}{2}$ For the medium semi-circle $r = 2a$. So $A = \frac{\pi r^2}{2} = \frac{\pi \times (2a)^2}{2} = \frac{\pi \times 2a \times 2a}{2} = \frac{4\pi a^2}{2}$ For the small semi-circle $r = a$. So $A = \frac{\pi r^2}{2} = \frac{\pi \times a^2}{2} = \frac{\pi a^2}{2}$ Then the total area of the shape is given by: $\frac{9\pi a^2}{2} + \frac{4\pi a^2}{2} - \frac{\pi a^2}{2} = 6\pi a^2$ • Remember to take away the area of the small semi-circle. • You would gain 2 marks if you found the areas of all three semi-circles (or circles) but did not obtain the correct answer. • You would gain 1 mark if you only found the area of the large semi-circle (or circle).	*Level 8 Algebra* *This question is testing the manipulation of algebraic formulae and equations.* See *Collins KS3 Maths Total Revision*, page 230 question 17

Part	Mark	Answer	Tutorial	What's this question looking for?
(b)	2	$a = \sqrt{\dfrac{2}{\pi}}$	• $6\pi a^2 = 12$ (Divide both sides by 6π) $a^2 = \dfrac{12}{6\pi} = \dfrac{2}{\pi}$ (Take the square root of both sides) $a = \sqrt{\dfrac{2}{\pi}}$ • You would only gain 1 mark if you tried to substitute 3.142 for π, since the question asks for the answer in terms of π.	
Total	**5**			

THIS IS THE END OF THE TIER 6–8 PAPER

Paper 2

Question 1

Part	Mark	Answer	Tutorial	What's this question looking for?
(a)	2	The completed form should look like this: 	Ben	20p
Cal	25p
Jan	30p
Kim	15p
Wyn	20p		• Make sure that you give Cal's amount as 25p and not as 25. • You can gain 1 mark if you get three out of the four entries correct.	*Level 3 Number* *This question is testing the use of a calculator and understanding of money notation.* **See *Collins KS3 Maths Total Revision*, page 6**
(b)	1	£1.10	• Use your calculator to work out 20 + 25 + 30 + 15 + 20. The answer is 110; this is in pence and must be changed to pounds to give £1.10.	
(c)	1	£20.25	• Use your calculator to work out 27×75. The answer is 2025. Again this is in pence and must be changed to pounds: 2025p = £20.25. If you are not sure how to do this in your head, you can divide 2025 by 100 on your calculator.	
(d)	1 1	£18 £4.50	• Use your calculator to work out 25×72. The answer is 1800. Again this is in pence and must be changed to pounds: 1800p = £18 or £18.00. • You could of course change 72p to pounds first: 72p = £0.72, and then work out 25×0.72. • To find a quarter of an amount, you just divide the amount by 4. Use your calculator to work out $18 \div 4$. The answer is 4.5. In pounds this must be written as £4.50. Don't forget to put the 0 at the end. Money answers in pounds must always have two places of decimals.	
Total	**6**			

Question 2

Part	Mark	Answer	Tutorial	What's this question looking for?
(a)	1	240 Yen	• It may help if you use column headings in this question: • 2 'lots' of 100, 4 'lots' of 10 and no units: H = 2, T = 4, U = 0	*Level 3 Number* *This question is testing place value with whole numbers.*
(b)	1	302 Yen	• Use column headings: 3 'lots' of 100, no 10s and 2 units: H = 3, T = 0, U = 2	**See *Collins KS3 Maths Total Revision*, page 5**
(c)	1	2513 Yen	• Use column headings: 2 'lots' of 1000, 5 'lots' of 100, 1 'lot' of 10 and 3 units: Th = 2, H = 5, T = 1, U = 3	
(d)	1	3052 Yen	• Use column headings: 3 'lots' of 1000, no 100s, 5 'lots' of 10 and 2 units: Th = 3, H = 0, T = 5, U = 2	
Total	4			

Question 3

Part	Mark	Answer	Tutorial	What's this question looking for?
(a)	1	4 boxes	• 1 can balances 2 boxes so 2 cans balance 4 boxes. Since 2 cans also balance 1 bottle, 4 boxes will also balance 1 bottle. This can be shown in a table. Can = 2, Bottle = 4 (Boxes)	*Level 3 Algebra* *This question is testing recognition of simple number patterns using symbols.*
(b)	1	5 boxes	• Using the table, 2 cans balance 4 boxes, so there are 5 boxes altogether.	
(c)	1	6 boxes	• Using the table, 1 bottle balances 4 boxes and 1 can balances 2 boxes, so there are 6 boxes altogether.	
(d)	1	 or boxes / can / bottle	• 1 bottle balances 4 boxes which is the same as 1 can and 2 boxes.	
Total	4			

Question 4

Part	Mark	Answer	Tutorial	What's this question looking for?
(a)	1	18 January	• The dates for the weeks go across the table 4, 11, 18. Be careful not to count the blank space at the beginning.	*Level 3 Handling data* *This question is testing skill in extracting information from tables.*
(b)	1 1	4 5	• It is not necessary to give the dates.	
(c)	1	… more Wednesdays (or Thursdays) than Sundays (or Mondays or Tuesdays or Fridays or Saturdays) …	• The list shows the 10 possible answers. You need to spot that there are five Wednesdays or Thursdays in April but only four of the other days. • Another answer could be '… more Wednesdays or Thursdays than any other days … '.	
(d)	1	11 February	• Count four weeks across the table from 14 January. You must give both the date and the month.	
(e)	1	3 weeks	• Counting across the table, this is 3 weeks. An answer of 2 weeks and 6 days is also acceptable. You must not give your answer in days only.	
(f)	1	Saturday	• The 7 times table is 7, 14, 21, 28. These dates appear on Saturdays in March.	
Total	7			

THIS IS THE START OF THE TIER 4–6 PAPER

Question 5

Part	Mark	Answer	Tutorial	What's this question looking for?
(a)	1	4	• The new pattern has four more tiles added each time: one to each corner. The question asks for the number of tiles added each time, so do not list the total number of tiles in each pattern. e.g. 4, 8, 12.	*Level 4 Number* *This question is testing knowledge of tables and describing number patterns.*
(b)	1	24	• Pattern 1 has 4 tiles, pattern 2 has 8 tiles and pattern 3 has 12 tiles. This is just your 4 times table, so pattern 6 has $6 \times 4 = 24$ tiles.	See *Collins KS3 Maths Total Revision*, page 17
(c)	1	36	• Use your 4 times table again. This is 9×4.	
(d)	1	10	• Be careful that you do a division here. $40 \div 4 = 10$	
Total	**4**			

Question 6

Part	Mark	Answer	Tutorial	What's this question looking for?
(a)	1	Spinner S	• This will be the spinner with the largest section (as a fraction of itself) which is plain. Half of spinner S is plain, the others are less than half plain.	*Level 4 Handling data* *This question is testing calculation of simple probability.*
(b)	1	Spinner R	• This will be the spinner with the smallest shaded section. Spinner R has no shaded section so the arrow has no chance of landing on 'shaded' and hence has the smallest probability.	See *Collins KS3 Maths Total Revision*, page 50
(c)	1	(shaded spinner diagram)	• To be certain that the arrow will land on 'shaded', the whole diagram will have to be shaded. Provided that you shade or colour the whole spinner you will gain 1 mark.	
(d)	1	(half-shaded spinner) or (spinner with striped half)	• A 50% chance means that you will need to shade half the spinner. You can leave the other half plain or have a mixture of plain and striped.	
Total	**4**			

Question 7

Part	Mark	Answer	Tutorial	What's this question looking for?
(a)	1	Liz	• Using Meg's sheet and counting the number of games each won: Jim won 3, Meg won 3, Liz won 4 and Bob won 2. Comparing this with Jim's sheet; Liz is missing 1 game. You will also gain 1 mark if you write Liz in the empty space in the table.	*Level 4 Handling data* *This question is testing skill in interpretation of data.* See *Collins KS3 Maths Total Revision*, page 41
(b)	1	Jim	• Using Jim's sheet, Bob won 1, Liz won 2 and Jim won 3. So Jim won the most games of Draughts.	
(c)	1	It tells you who won the most games overall. – *or* – It's quick and easy to fill in.	• Always make your answer clear; a short answer is best. Do not give vague answers which could apply to either table, such as 'It is easy to use' or 'It is better'.	
(d)	1	It tells you who won each separate game. – *or* – You are less likely to make mistakes as you fill it in.	• This table is showing you who won each separate game and so contains more detailed information; it does not show you who played whom at each game.	
Total	4			

THIS IS THE START OF THE TIER 5-7 PAPER

Question 8

Part	Mark	Answer	Tutorial	What's this question looking for?
(a)	1	The completed column should be: 400 300 300 200 100	• To round to the nearest 100, you first look at the number in the tens column to see if the number is under or over 50. For example, 354 is over 350 and so is nearer to 400 but 346 is under 350 and so is nearer to 300. If the number is exactly 50, such as 350, it is usual to round up, in this case to 400.	*Level 5 Number* *This question is testing ability to round numbers to the nearest 10 or 100.* See *Collins KS3 Maths Total Revision,* page 72
	1	Thames and Trent		
(b)	1	The completed column should be: 350 350 300 220 110	• To round to the nearest 10, you look at the units column to see if the number is over or under 5. 354 is under 355 and so is nearer to 350. 346 is over 345 and so is nearer to 350. If the number is exactly halfway, such as 215, it is usual to round up, in this case to 220 but you would not lose a mark if you rounded down to 210.	
	1	Severn and Thames		
(c)	1	Any one of the following numbers: 150 or 151 or 152 or 153 or 154 or 155	• If the river is 200 km long to the nearest 100 km, then its length must lie between 150 km and 250 km. If it is 150 km long to the nearest 10 km, then its length must lie between 145 km and 155 km. Any of the given numbers fit both of these conditions. • Since the question states that the answer is to the nearest km, only whole numbers should be used.	
(d)	2	Any one of the following numbers: 245 or 246 or 247 or 248 or 249 or 250, and any one of the following numbers: 250 or 251 or 252 or 253 or 254 or 255, but 250 cannot be repeated.	• If the river is 250 km to the nearest 10 km, its length can lie between 245 km and 255 km. If the length of the river is different to the nearest 100 km, then if it is above 250 km it will be nearer to 300 km and if it is below 250 km it will be nearer to 200 km. Any of the numbers given fit both of these conditions but you cannot repeat 250.	
Total	7			

Question 9

Part	Mark	Answer	Tutorial	What's this question looking for?
(a)	1		• Congruent shapes are shapes that are exactly the same although they may be in different positions. There is only one way to make a rectangle using the two congruent triangles. Your drawing need not be totally accurate provided your intention is clear.	*Level 4 Shape, space and measures* *This question is testing skill in identifying congruent shapes.* **See Collins KS3 Maths Total Revision, page 34**
(b)	1		• You may find it helpful to trace the triangle. Remember that you can turn over your tracing, since it will still be congruent to the triangle. Using your tracing will ensure that the triangle you add is congruent to the original triangle.	**Note:** Question 9 does not appear on the Tier 5–7 Paper.
(c)	1		• You must make a different triangle. The answers to (b) and (c) can be interchanged.	
Total	**3**			

Question 10

Part	Mark	Answer	Tutorial	What's this question looking for?
(a)	2	6 litres of red and 14 litres of blue	• For purple you need $3 + 7 = 10$ parts. So for $20\,l$ of purple paint there will be $2\,l$ for each part. The amount of red $= 3 \times 2 = 6\,l$, the amount of blue $= 7 \times 2 = 14\,l$. If you give any other answer in the ratio $3 : 7$, e.g. 30 and 70 or 60 and 140, you will gain 1 mark.	*Level 5 Number* *This question is testing use of simple ratio.* **See Collins KS3 Maths Total Revision, page 118**
(b)	2	6.5 litres of yellow and 3.5 litres of red	• For orange you need $13 + 7 = 20$ parts. So for $10\,l$ of orange paint there will be $\frac{1}{2}\,l$ for each part. Amount of yellow $= 13 \times \frac{1}{2} = 6\frac{1}{2}\,l$, amount of red $= 7 \times \frac{1}{2} = 3\frac{1}{2}\,l$. You will gain 1 mark if you have an answer in the correct ratio, even if it is not the same as the one given, e.g. 130 and 70.	
Total	**4**			

Question 11

Part	Mark	Answer	Tutorial	What's this question looking for?
(a)	1	Any of these diagrams is suitable, and there are others that will be similar to these.	● Always check your answer, using tracing paper or a mirror. The two triominoes do not have to touch but they must not overlap. The internal lines showing the individual squares of the triominoes do not have to be shown. You will not gain a mark if you use the shape given in the question.	*Level 5 Shape, space and measures* *This question is testing recognition of reflective and rotational symmetry.* **See Collins KS3 Maths Total Revision, page 85**
(b)	1	Any of these diagrams is suitable, and there are others that will be similar to these.	● You don't have to draw the lines of symmetry on the shape, but check the lines of symmetry, using tracing paper or a mirror.	
(c)	1	Any of these diagrams is suitable, and there are others that will be similar to these.	● You can use any shape that you have drawn before. Again, check your answer using tracing paper or a mirror.	

Part	Mark	Answer	Tutorial	What's this question looking for?
(d)	1	Any of these diagrams is suitable, and there are others that will be similar to these.	● You will be allowed to use any shape that you have drawn before.	
Total	4			

Question 12

Part	Mark	Answer	Tutorial	What's this question looking for?
(a)	1	Any percentage from 20% to 30% inclusive.	● The section for people in Greece aged 40–59 is about $\frac{1}{4}$ of the circle. This is about 25%. Any answer from 20% to 30% inclusive would be acceptable.	*Level 5 Handling data* *This question is testing skill in interpretation of pie charts.* See *Collins KS3 Maths Total Revision*, page 96
(b)	1	Any number from 2 million to 3 million inclusive.	● Use your answer to part (a). e.g. 25% of 10 = $\frac{25}{100} \times 10 = 2.5$ or $\frac{1}{4}$ of 10 is $2\frac{1}{2}$. Notice that the million is already on the answer line, so be careful not to write your answer as 2 500 000 million.	
(c)	1	Greece has a larger population. – *or* – The total populations are not the same. – *or* – Pie charts only show proportions.	● A pie chart only shows proportions, so does not tell you the number of people in each country.	

Part	Mark	Answer	Tutorial	What's this question looking for?
(d)	2 1	**UK** over 59 / under 15 / 40–59 / 15–39 60 million people	• The four sections of the pie chart can be drawn in any order. There are 10 sections on the pie chart, so each section is worth 10%. Shade 2 sections for 20%, $3\frac{1}{2}$ sections for 35%, $2\frac{1}{2}$ sections for 25% and 2 sections for 20%. You will gain 2 marks for a correct pie chart. You will gain 1 mark if you draw two sections that are the correct size, provided that your pie chart has four sections. • It is a good idea to shade each of the four sectors differently. • Remember to label each sector of the pie chart with the correct ages. You do not have to show the percentages. You gain 1 mark if the labels are placed correctly on the pie chart.	
Total	**6**			

Question 13

Part	Mark	Answer	Tutorial	What's this question looking for?
(a)	1	✔	• The correct net should be ticked. When choosing the correct net it may help to think about wrapping a label around a tin.	*Level 5 Shape, space and measures* *This question is testing skill in drawing accurate nets for 3-D shapes.* See *Collins KS3 Maths Total Revision,* page 31
(b)	2	The semi-circle should have a radius of 4 cm. This diagram must be exact. The one shown on the right is half-size.	• Draw the diameter of 8 cm first and then set your compasses to a radius of 4 cm to complete the semi-circle.	
Total	**3**			

THIS IS THE END OF THE TIER 3–5 PAPER

THIS IS THE START OF THE TIER 6–8 PAPER

Question 14

Part	Mark	Answer	Tutorial	What's this question looking for?
(a)	1	$\frac{35}{36}$ or 0.97	• The probability of an event not happening is 1 minus the probability of the event happening. We usually write this as: P(not event) = 1 – P(event) or P(A') = 1 – P(A) where A' means the event 'not A'. You can work out $1 - \frac{1}{36}$ on a calculator but it is easy enough to do mentally as all you have to do is work out 36 – 1 to find the new numerator (top number). You must work out the answer to get the mark. The decimal is $35 \div 36 = 0.972\,222\,2$ rounded off. You can also give a probability as a percentage, i.e. 97% but you must not give it as a ratio, e.g. 35 : 36 or in words, e.g. 35 out of 36 or 35 in 36.	*Level 6 Handling data* **This question is testing knowledge of complementary events and combined events.** See *Collins KS3 Maths Total Revision,* page 161
(b)	1	Tick the $\frac{1}{36}$ box and give an acceptable explanation.	• Every time you throw the dice, this is a fresh event, so the probabilities remain the same. If you threw two dice and scored three double sixes in a row, it is natural to think that it couldn't happen again but as far as the dice are concerned it is still a $\frac{1}{36}$ chance. These are known as independent events. i.e. the outcome of one event does not determine the outcome of another. The simplest answer would be 'The probability does not change', the best mathematical answer would be 'The events are independent'. There is no need to write lengthy explanations. Keep them short and relevant. Sometimes long explanations can even cause you to lose a mark if you write down something that is wrong. For example 'The chance is the same, it is evens' would get no marks because evens means a probability of $\frac{1}{2}$ or 50%.	
(c)	1	$\frac{1}{36}$ or 0.027 or 0.028 or 2.7% or 2.8%	• The chance of a double 3 is the same as the chance of a double six. Note that decimals and percentages are acceptable, either truncated or rounded, but probability is usually expressed as a fraction.	

95

Part	Mark	Answer	Tutorial	What's this question looking for?
(d)	1	$\frac{6}{36}$ or $\frac{1}{6}$	• There are six possible doubles, each having the same chance ($\frac{1}{36}$) $6 \times \frac{1}{36} = \frac{6}{36}$ or $\frac{1}{6}$ This fraction cancels down but you would not lose marks if you did not cancel. Look out for the words 'give your answer in its simplest form' or 'give your answer as simply as possible'. If this is what it says in the question, then you are expected to cancel and you would lose marks if you did not.	
Total	4			

Question 15

Part	Mark	Answer	Tutorial	What's this question looking for?
(a)	1	South America	• The problem is to work out 12% of 148 355. This is found as $12 \times 148\,355 \div 100$ or $12 \div 100 \times 148\,355 = 17\,802.6$. The only number near this is 17 793, which is the area of South America.	*Level 6–7 Number* *This question involves percentages.* See *Collins KS3 Maths Total Revision,* pages 111 and 176
(b)	2	8.9% or 9%	• The calculation needed in this question is $13\,209 \div 148\,355 \times 100 = 8.903\,643\,288\,1$. It is sensible to round this off to 8.9 or 9. You can gain 1 mark if you show the division but make a mistake such as forgetting to multiply by 100, which is why it is always worth showing working even though you will probably do this entirely on your calculator.	
(c)	2	500	• The calculation is $150 \div 30 \times 100 = 500$. You could work out $148\,355 \div 30 \times 100 = 495\,416.7$ but the question only asks for approximate answers. You can also get confused by the units: the table is in 1000 km^2 units but the area in (c) is in million km^2 units. You can gain 1 mark for a complete method and a wrong answer. • This question is a good example of the three types of percentage problem. The first part requires a percentage of a quantity, the second requires one quantity as a percentage of another and the third requires 100%, given the percentage represented by a quantity. There are only three types of percentage problem. You will need to learn how to solve all three if you are working at level 7 and the first two if you are working at level 6.	*This is a reverse percentage problem.* **Note:** Only parts (a) and (b) of question 15 are in the Tier 4–6 Paper. Therefore the total mark for this question in Tiers 4–6 is 3. Part (c) is in the Tiers 5–7 and 6–8 Papers. Therefore the total mark for this question in Tiers 5–7 and 6–8 is 5.
Total	5			

Question 16

Part	Mark	Answer	Tutorial	What's this question looking for?
	2	Correct shape in correct orientation with no redundant or missing lines. i.e. or	• This is a question about the two-dimensional representation of three-dimensional shapes. It is also called isometric drawing. Normally you are given a grid on which to draw the shapes. Only ever draw lines in three directions: • If you draw horizontal lines or lines in other directions you will find it impossible to draw the required pictures. For example: • It might look all right but it will not score any marks. You also have to use your imagination to work out how the shape will look. You can still gain 1 mark if you draw the correct shape but in the wrong position. For example these all gain 1 mark. • You must be careful when you draw these shapes not to put in lines for sides that you cannot see or leave out lines for edges of cubes that you can see. These would both gain 1 mark:	*Level 6 Shape, space and measures* *This question involves isometric drawing and the properties of 3-D shapes.* See Collins KS3 Maths Total Revision, page 137
Total	2			

Question 17

Part	Mark	Answer	Tutorial	What's this question looking for?
(a)	2	65	• The mean score is an average that is calculated as total score ÷ number of matches. A mean score of 60 over three games is a total score of 180 for all three games. In the first two games Jeff scores $62 + 53 = 115$, so he needs to score $180 - 115 = 65$ in the last game. You can also say at least 65 because Jeff can get a mean of over 65. • You can score 1 mark for a correct method or for mentioning 180 in your working.	*Level 6 Handling data* *This question is testing understanding of correlation and scatter diagrams.* See Collins KS3 Maths Total Revision, page 158

Part	Mark	Answer	Tutorial	What's this question looking for?
(b)	1	30 and 50 in any order	• The mean is total score ÷ 3. Range is highest score – lowest score. Nia's mean is $(35 + 40 + 45) ÷ 3 = 120 ÷ 3 = 40$ and her range is $45 - 35 = 10$. Imran needs two scores that add up to 80 so that the total is still 120. They also need a difference of 20 to make the range 20. It is easy to see they must be 30 and 50.	
(c)	2	Positive relationship and no relationship. i.e. A and B  ☑ A and C  ☑	• These scatter diagrams illustrate the various possibilities. Perfect positive relationship / Positive relationship / No relationship / Negative relationship / Perfect negative relationship 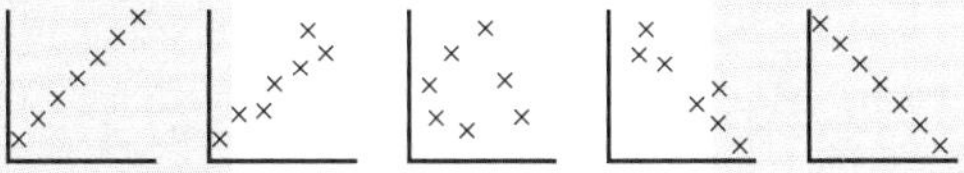 • You can see that the scores of people on game A and game B (first graph) have a positive relationship. Putting it into words: 'People who score well on game A also score well on game B' *or* 'There is positive correlation between the scores on game A and game B'. • The second graph shows that there is no relationship between the scores in game A and the scores in game C. Putting it into words: 'There is no correlation between the scores in game A and game C.'	*This part is about correlation, or the connection between two variables on a scatter diagram.*
(d)	1	no relationship B and C  ☑	• If there is a positive relationship between A and B and no relationship between A and C then there will be no relationship between B and C. This means that someone who is good at game A is also good at game B but may or may not be good at game C. • You can still score on this part of the question if your answer to (d) is the same as your answer to the last part of (c), provided you do not give an unacceptable answer for the first part of (c). These are acceptable, for example: 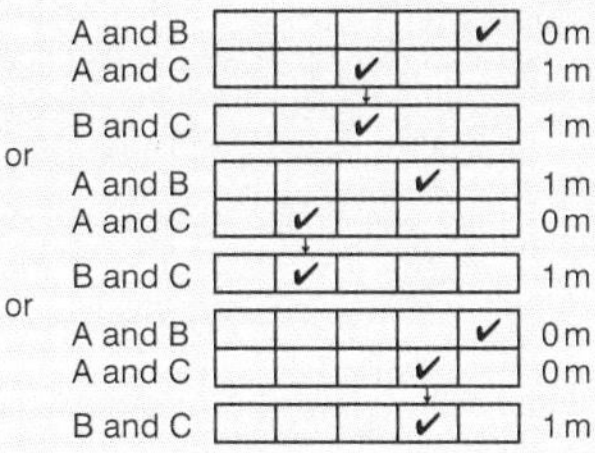 A and B ☑ 0m A and C ☑ 1m B and C ☑ 1m or A and B ☑ 1m A and C ☑ 0m B and C ☑ 1m or A and B ☑ 0m A and C ☑ 0m B and C ☑ 1m	
Total	6			

Question 18

Part	Mark	Answer	Tutorial	What's this question looking for?
(a)	2	60	• There are several ways of working out the area of this shape. The most obvious is to work out the area of one triangle and then multiply this by 6. Area of one triangle = $\frac{1}{2} \times 4 \times 5 = 10$ Total = $6 \times 10 = 60$ Another common way would be to work out the area of the outside rectangle and then subtract the four triangles at each corner. Rectangle = 8×10 Corner triangle = $\frac{1}{2} \times 2.5 \times 4 = 5$ Total area = $80 - (4 \times 5) = 60$ Other methods are to make the shape into two rectangles by rotating two half-triangles from the bottom to the top. Area of top rectangle = $4 \times 10 = 40$ Area of bottom rectangle = $5 \times 4 = 20$ Total area = $40 + 20 = 60$ You can also think of the shape as two trapezia, work out the area of one of them and double it. Area of one trapezium = $\frac{1}{2} \times 4 \times (5 + 10) = 30$ Total = $2 \times 30 = 60$ • You can gain 1 mark by using a correct method but making one error, or by showing a method for finding the area of one of the small triangles. e.g. $4 \times 5 \div 2 = 10$	*Level 6–7 Shape, space and measures* *This question involves calculation of volumes of prisms and compound measures such as density.* See *Collins KS3 Maths Total Revision*, pages 147 and 206 **Note:** The Tier 4–6 Paper includes parts (a) and (b) but not part (c) of question 18.

Part	Mark	Answer	Tutorial	What's this question looking for?
(b)	3	Follow through from (a). i.e. if (a) is 60 this answer is 240 cm³.	• There are three steps to finding the correct answer. 1 Find the volume of the prism (total volume of box). 2 Find 80% of the volume (total volume of coffee). 3 Multiply the volume of coffee by 0.5 to find the number of grams of coffee. These steps can be done in any order but the sequence above is most sensible. Each step gains 1 mark. • The volume of a prism is given in the formulae as: volume = area of cross section × length volume = answer to (a) × 10 = 60 × 10 = 600 cm³ • The volume of coffee in the box is 80% of (your volume) = 80% of 600 = 480 cm³ • Mass of coffee is 0.5 × (your volume of coffee) = 0.5 × 480 = 240 grams • If you carry out any two steps you will gain 2 marks. If you carry out any one step you gain 1 mark. • The most common error on this question was to double the volume of coffee to get the mass (e.g. 480 ÷ 0.5 = 960 grams). Pupils who showed this working would gain 2 marks. Pupils who put down no working would gain no marks because the examiner does not know where the answer came from.	*This is an example of an unstructured question. These will become more common in SATs in future. An unstructured question is one where you have to take more than one step to get the answer. It is always worth showing lots of working in this sort of question, as you will gain some marks for working even if your final answer is wrong.* The total mark for question 18 in Tiers 4–6 is 5.
Total	**5**			

THIS IS THE END OF THE TIER 4–6 PAPER

Question 18 (continued)

Part	Mark	Answer	Tutorial	What's this question looking for?
(c)	2	£0.96 or £0.97	• The clue to the calculation you need to do is given in the wording of the question. The key phrase is per 100 g. This means you will divide by the weight. The basic calculation is therefore 2.19 ÷ 227 but this is per gram. To get 'per 100 grams' you must multiply this by 100. Alternatively you can find 219 ÷ 227 straight away.	*This part of the question is testing manipulation of units and compound measures.* See *Collins KS3 Maths Total Revision,* page 206 The total mark for question 18 in Tiers 5–7 and 6–8 is 7.
Total	**7**			

Question 19

Part	Mark	Answer	Tutorial	What's this question looking for?
(a)	3	No, with a complete justification.	• There are several ways to answer this question. Almost all of them will involve calculating the circumference of the table. The formula for this is given at the start of the paper i.e. $C = 2\pi r$. You may also know it as $C = \pi d$. This is $2 \times \pi \times 2.75$ or $\pi \times 5.5 = 17.27$ metres. From here the most common methods would be: (i) Convert to centimetres and divide by 50 to find the space each person has. $1727 \div 50 = 34.54$ cm. This is less than 45 cm so there is not enough space. (ii) Divide the circumference by 45 to find out how many people can sit round the table. $1727 \div 45 = 38.4$ which is less than 50 so there is not enough space. (iii) Compare how much space 50 people need. $50 \times 45 = 2250$ which is bigger than 1727 so there is not enough space. • For each error you make, 1 mark is deducted. The most common errors are: • calculating the wrong radius e.g. $5.5 \div 2 = 2.25$ • using the diameter as the radius, circumference $= 2 \times \pi \times 5.5$ • using wrong units (metres not centimetres) • making an arithmetic error • not making a comparison. The only other method that would be acceptable is to calculate the diameter needed for a table that could sit 50 people. e.g. $50 \times 45 = 2250$, $2250 \div \pi = 7.16$ metres, more than 5.5 m.	*Level 7 Shape, space and measures* ▸ *This question involves the area and circumference of a circle.* **See Collins KS3 Maths Total Revision, page 147**
(b)	3	18.84–18.86 m^2	• There is only one way to do this problem. Work out the area of the inner circle and subtract it from the area of the larger circle. The formula for the area of a circle is given at the start of the paper i.e. $A = \pi r^2$. • For this you will need the radius of the inner circle. This is 1.25 m (2.75 – 1.5). The calculation is then $\pi \times 2.75^2 - \pi \times 1.25^2 = 18.85$. The answer could also be left as 6π or it could be rounded or truncated to 18.8, 18.9 or 19. • You can gain 2 marks for showing the correct method but working it out incorrectly. You can gain 1 mark by working out the area of the large circle (23.75) or finding the radius of the inner circle (1.25).	*This is another example of an unstructured question (see comments at end of question 18).*
Total	**6**			

Question 20

Part	Mark	Answer	Tutorial	What's this question looking for?
(a)	1	Sue and a correct explanation.	• The probability worked out from an experiment is known as relative frequency or experimental probability. The more experiments are conducted, the nearer the relative frequency gets to the real (theoretical) probability. You should therefore pick Sue and say something like 'She had the most throws.'	*Level 7–8 Handling data* *This question tests understanding of relative (experimental) and theoretical probability.* See *Collins KS3 Maths Total Revision,* page 222
(b)	1	$\frac{171}{300}$, 0.57 or 57%	• Out of a total of $171 + 120 + 9 = 300$ throws altogether, there were 171 throws that were 'all different'. This is a basic definition of probability. • P(event) = number of outcomes that give the event ÷ number of possible outcomes altogether	
(c)	2	167, 125 and 8	• The theoretical probability is what you would expect in a perfect world. So in 300 throws you would expect the number of times each event occurs to be equal to its theoretical probability multiplied by 300. These actually give answers of 166.6666, 125 and 8.3333. The answers are rounded off but other combinations are possible. You can have 166, 125, 9 or 166.7, 125, 8.3. The total of the answers must be 300. If you put 166, 125 and 8 you would only gain 1 mark. Answers as fractions with a denominator of 300 are acceptable for 2 marks but percentages (56%, 42% and 2% or 56%, 41% and 3%) would only gain 1 mark.	
(d)	1	Any acceptable explanation such as 'Experimental results are random.'	• You have to show that you realise the difference between experimental probability and theoretical probability, or that as the number of throws increases the experimental probability gets closer to the theoretical probability. Any of the following explanations would gain the mark: • The pupils haven't thrown the dice enough times. • They need to do more throws to get them closer. • It's random. • Every time you do the experiment you could throw different results.	

Part	Mark	Answer	Tutorial	What's this question looking for?
(e)	2	$\frac{1}{1296}$, 0.000 77, 0.077%	• To get 'all the same' both times you need to throw 'all the same' the first time and 'all the same' the second time. Whenever independent events are linked by the word 'and' it means that you multiply the probabilities of each event together. The probability of 'all the same' is $\frac{1}{36}$ so to do this twice is $\frac{1}{36} \times \frac{1}{36} = \frac{1}{1296}$. • Answers can be given as decimals or percentages but fractions are better, although most calculators with a fraction button will not give answers with four digits in the denominator. You will probably get 7.71^{-04} or 7.71 -04 in your display. This is standard form and comes up in question 25 on Paper 1. You can gain 1 mark for using the wrong probabilities and the right method or the right probabilities and getting the wrong answer.	**Note:** Part (e) of question 20 only appears in the Tier 6–8 Paper. Therefore the total mark for this question in Tiers 5–7 is 5.
Total	**7**			

Question 21

Part	Mark	Answer	Tutorial	What's this question looking for?
(a)	2	8.9 to 8.91	• This is Pythagoras' theorem. The formula for this is given at the start of the paper. i.e. For a right-angled triangle $a^2 + b^2 = c^2$ (Pythagoras' theorem) The triangle in the question is not orientated in the same way but you are looking for a hypotenuse so the calculation is: $x^2 = 7.5^2 + 4.8^2$ (where x is the distance required) $x^2 = 79.29$ $x = 8.9$ • There is always a question on Pythagoras' theorem in every SATs paper. It is level 7. You should learn to recognise Pythagoras' theorem and how to use it. There are only two basic problems – finding the hypotenuse (the long side) and finding a short side. To find a short side you have to use $a^2 = c^2 - b^2$. In each case do not forget to take the square root when you have worked out the first part of the calculation.	*Level 7–8 Shape, space and measures* *This question involves Pythagoras' theorem and trigonometry.* See *Collins KS3 Maths Total Revision,* page 195

Part	Mark	Answer	Tutorial	What's this question looking for?
(b)	2	56° to 56.5°	• This is trigonometry. There are three trigonometric ratios, which are given in the tables at the start of the paper. i.e. For a right-angled triangle: $a = c \cos x \qquad \cos x = \dfrac{a}{c}$ $b = c \sin x \qquad \sin x = \dfrac{b}{c}$ $b = a \tan x \qquad \tan x = \dfrac{b}{a}$ Each ratio connects two sides. In this question we have the opposite side (side b) and the adjacent side (side a). This involves the tangent ratio. $\tan x = \frac{6}{4} \qquad x = 56.3°$ • You also have to identify which angle is required. A bearing is measured from north in a clockwise direction. Bearings should always be given in three figures, so you can give an answer of 056.3°, for example. There is a lot to do in this question for 2 marks. However, it is level 8. Not many pupils do level 8 so you will probably not have been taught how to do trigonometry. • You can gain one mark for showing a correct method and the wrong answer (e.g. 0.078 985 comes from keying [6] [÷] [4] [tan⁻¹] instead of [6] [÷] [4] [=] [tan⁻¹] which is the correct key sequence on most calculators).	*This part of the question involves trigonometry.* See *Collins KS3 Maths Total Revision*, page 232 question 13 **Note:** Parts (b) and (c) of question 21 only appear in the Tier 6–8 Paper. Therefore the total mark for this question in Tiers 5–7 is 2.
(c)	3	1.4 km	• This is quite a complicated trigonometry question. It requires you to draw a diagram to see what is going on. • The distance y is worked out by $y = 6 \div \tan 48° = 5.4024$ The distance required is $y - 4 = 5.4024 - 4$ $= 1.4$ km. There are other ways of solving the problem, such as similar triangles or the sine rule but these require some extra information to be found so the method above is the most straightforward.	
Total	**7**			

Question 22

Part	Mark	Answer	Tutorial	What's this question looking for?
(a)	2	13	• This is a percentage question. If the birth rate fell by 26.1% then the actual birth rate in 1994 is $100 - 26.1 = 73.9\%$ of what it was in 1961. Once you have worked this out the calculation is quite straightforward. i.e. $17.6 \times 73.9 \div 100 = 13.0064$	*Level 7–8 Number* *This question is about percentages and applying mathematics to real problems.*
(b)	2	28 or a value between 28.2 and 28.3	• The fall in the birth rate is $17.0 - 12.2 = 4.8$. The problem is then to work out what percentage 4.8 is of 17.0. The calculation is $4.8 \div 17.0 \times 100 = 28.2\%$.	See *Collins KS3 Maths Total Revision,* pages 111 and 176 Parts (a) and (b) are very similar to parts (a) and (b) of question 15. These are slightly more difficult because extra interpretation is needed to work out what calculation to do. The total mark for question 22 in Tiers 5–7 is 4.
Total	**4**			

THIS IS THE END OF THE TIER 5-7 PAPER

Question 22 (continued)

Part	Mark	Answer	Tutorial	What's this question looking for?
(c)	1	⬜ ⬜ ✓ ⬜	• This is a difficult question to interpret. Often the best way to do this is to make up numbers for the birth rates in Scotland and Northern Ireland and see what happens. For example, take the birth rate in Scotland to be 100, and in Northern Ireland to be 50. (It does not matter if the numbers are not sensible.) Let them both drop by the same amount, say 10. That means that 10 out of 100 for Scotland is 10% and that 10 out of 50 for Northern Ireland is 20%. You can see that the percentage fall in Scotland is greater than in Northern Ireland. Try the numbers the other way round and it is clear that the third statement is true.	**Note:** Part (c) of question 22 only appears in the Tier 6–8 Paper. The total mark for question 22 in Tiers 6–8 is 5.
Total	**5**			

Question 23

Part	Mark	Answer	Tutorial	What's this question looking for?
(a)	1	Median: any value between 0.62 and 0.63 m	• These questions are very common in SATs. The diagram is called a cumulative frequency diagram. For example as the graph passes through the point (0.65, 100), this means that there are 100 trees with a height below 0.65 m. The median is read from the middle of the cumulative frequency scale. A line is drawn from 75 on the vertical (side) axis across to the graph and down to the bottom axis (see diagram below). This gives a value of about 0.625. This does not have to be highly accurate as you are reading from a graph. The median shows that half of the trees have a height below 0.625 m.	*Level 8 Handling data* *This question is testing understanding of cumulative frequency.* See *Collins KS3 Maths Total Revision,* page 234 question 15
	2	Interquartile range: any value between 0.07 and 0.1	• The interquartile range is found by reading across from the quarter and three-quarter values of the cumulative frequency scale. These are at 37.5 and 112.5. Reading across to the graph and down to the bottom axis from these values gives a 'lower quartile' of about 0.58 and an 'upper quartile' of about 0.67. The interquartile range is found by subtracting. $0.67 - 0.58 = 0.09$ • You can gain 1 mark by showing a correct method to calculate the inter-quartile range but getting the answer wrong. 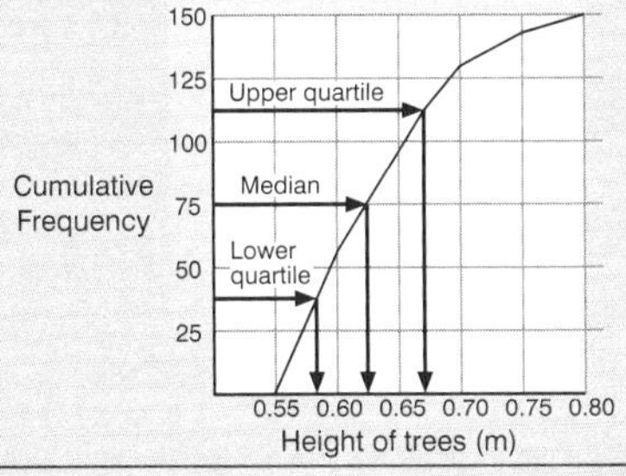	
(b)	1	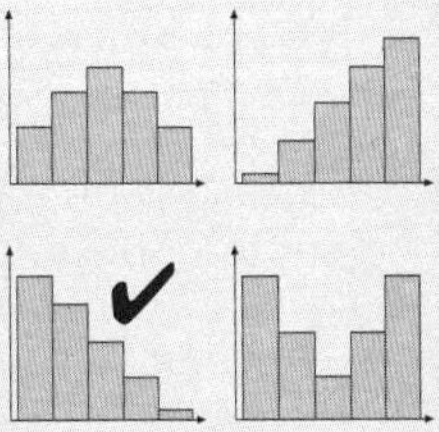	• The frequency distribution is found by 'undoing' the cumulative frequency diagram. If you look at this you can see that the following table would be about correct 	Height of trees	Frequency	 |---|---| 	$0.55 \leqslant h < 0.60$	56	 	$0.60 \leqslant h < 0.65$	44	 	$0.65 \leqslant h < 0.70$	29	 	$0.70 \leqslant h < 0.75$	16	 	$0.75 \leqslant h < 0.80$	5	 • The frequency diagram that fits this data is the one on the bottom left.	
Total	4			

Question 24

Part	Mark	Answer	Tutorial	What's this question looking for?
(a)	2	28 cm	• The clue to this question is the word 'similar' in the introduction. This means that the sides or dimensions of each pot are in the same ratio, i.e. the heights of each pot are in the same ratio as the diameters, or the ratio of the height of each pot to its diameter is the same. The easiest way to do this is to set up an equation using fractions (fractions are more or less the same as ratios and are much easier to work with). The following is a possible equation. $\frac{m}{42} = \frac{40}{60}$ This is solved by cross-multiplying to take 42 to the other side: $m = \frac{40 \times 42}{60}$ $m = 28$ • Another equation would be: $\frac{m}{40} = \frac{42}{60}$ • You could also see that the large pot is $1\frac{1}{2}$ times as big as the smaller pot. • You can gain 1 mark if you set up the right equation, or show the scale factor of $1\frac{1}{2}$ or $\frac{2}{3}$.	*Level 8 Number* *This part of the question involves similarity.* See *Collins KS3 Maths Total Revision*, page 232 question 12
(b)	3	77.5–78 inclusive	• This question is about substituting numbers into a complicated formula. You also need to know that there are 1000 cubic centimetres in a litre. The calculation is: $C = \frac{1}{12} \times \pi \times 42 \times (60^2 + 60 \times 36 + 36^2)$ This gives $C = \frac{1}{12} \times \pi \times 42 \times (3600 + 2160 + 1296)$ This gives $C = \frac{1}{12} \times \pi \times 42 \times 7056$ $C = 77\,584.77$ cubic centimetres $C = 77.6$ litres • You can gain 2 marks by giving the answer in cubic centimetres. You can gain 1 mark by partially evaluating the calculation, e.g. getting 7056.	*This part of the question is about substituting into formulae.* See *Collins KS3 Maths Total Revision*, page 229 questions 3 and 4
(c)	1	A correct explanation	• If two objects are similar then the scale factor between two corresponding lengths is called the linear scale factor. The areas are then in the ratio (linear scale factor)^2 and the volumes are in the ratio (linear scale factor)^3. Comparing the diameters, the linear scale factor is 40 : 60 which cancels to 2 : 3. The volume scale factor is $2^3 : 3^3 = 8 : 27$.	*This part of the question is about scale factors.*
Total	6			

THIS IS THE END OF THE TIER 6–8 PAPER

Mental arithmetic tests

Mental arithmetic test C (Lower tier)

Each question is worth 1 mark only.

Number	Answer	Tutorial	Collins KS3 Maths Total Revision
1	Rectangle	You should have a picture like this in your mind.	Shape and symmetry, pages 31 and 33
2	2028	Two thousand and twenty-eight does not have a 'hundreds' number in it so the second digit must be zero.	Place value, page 5
3	100 cm	You need to know your metric units and their relationships.	Metric units, page 87
4	$28.5 <$ answer < 29. e.g. 28.6, 28.9	Any number between 28.5 and 29 will do but it cannot include 28.5 or 29.	
5	63	You need to know your tables.	Multiplication tables, page 1
6	22	If $6y = 66$ then $2y$ is one-third of this, so $2y = 22$. You could also work out that $y = 11$ and then double it.	Solving simple equations, page 124
7	7.32	$732 \div 100 = 7.32$. When you divide by 100 all the digits move to the right by two places. You may think of this as moving the decimal point 2 places to the left.	Multiplying and dividing by 10 and 100, page 5
8	£4.20	$4 \times £1.05$. This is best done by calculating $4 \times £1 = £4$ and $4 \times 5p = 20p$, then adding the answers together.	
9	37	You need to combine 12 and 18 to give 30 and then add 7 to 30 to get 37.	
10	You should tick this spinner (the bottom left).	The spinner which is most likely to land on grey is the one with the largest grey area. The top left spinner has half of its area shaded grey, the top right has a quarter shaded and the bottom right has half shaded. The correct spinner has about five-eighths shaded.	Probability, page 99
11	13	$21 - n = 8$ has a solution of $n = 13$ because $21 - 13 = 8$.	Solving equations, page 124
12	7900	$8000 - 100 = 7900$. This is a fairly straightforward calculation but you have to realise that the problem is a subtraction.	
13	$23\% \leqslant$ answer $\leqslant 27\%$. e.g. 25%	It should be clear that a quarter of the pie chart is allocated to pupils who cycle to school. 25% is the obvious answer as $25\% = \frac{1}{4}$.	Pie charts, page 96 Equivalent fractions, page 114

Number	Answer	Tutorial	*Collins KS3 Maths Total Revision*
14	9	You should have a picture like this (either in your mind or drawn on the paper). It is clear that the answer is 9 small squares.	
15	£33	This is the calculation £52 – £19. The easy way to do this mentally is to take away £20 first: £52 – £20 = £32 and then add on £1: £32 + £1 = £33.	
16	£3.02	First of all you have to work out the cost of 2 pens. 2 × £3.49 = £6.98. The easy way to do this is 2 × £3.50 = £7 then subtract 2p. This has to be taken away from £10. 2p makes it up to £7 and £10 – £7 = £3. So the answer is £3.02.	
17	5 hours	You need to know that there are 60 minutes in an hour. Then you have to calculate $300 \div 60 = 5$. No problem if you know your 60 times table! Actually all you need is your 6 times table.	
18	⁻12	It is easy to get this the wrong way round. Subtract 20 from 8 means $8 - 20 = {}^{-}12$.	Directed numbers, page 61
19	10 cm	You need to know that an equilateral triangle has three equal sides. $30 \div 3 = 10$	
20	33 years	The calculation is 1920 – 1887, but this is not easy to do mentally. If you 'count on' from 1887 to 1900 and then from 1900 to 1920 you get $13 + 20 = 33$. You could also have said 32 or 34 years as the author could have moved in or moved out at the very start or very end of a year!	
21	10	You should know about BODMAS, which tells you to do the bracket first. $30 \div (6 - 3)$ becomes $30 \div 3 = 10$.	BODMAS, page 172
22	8 km	You are expected to know some of the basic conversions. One of these is that 5 miles ≈ 8 kilometres.	Conversion factors, page 88
23	£33	10% of 30 is the same as $\frac{1}{10}$ of 30. This is £3. £30 + £3 = £33.	Percentages, page 64

Number	Answer	Tutorial	*Collins KS3 Maths Total Revision*
24	You should have ticked the parallelogram.	All of the other shapes have at least 1 line of symmetry.	Symmetry, page 33
25	7 minutes	The train leaves Tarn at 10:38 and gets to Barham at 10:45. This is 7 minutes. Time problems can be a bit tricky as you cannot use a calculator to solve them and there are not 100 minutes in an hour. This problem is quite easy though and if you had used a calculator you would have found that $1045 - 1038 = 7$!	
26	You should imagine doing this with the square: triangle rectangle	You should know the properties of polygons.	Polygons, page 31
27	You should have circled 0.02.	To put decimals in order you need to write each one with the same number of decimal places. This gives the numbers as 0.20, 0.20, 0.28, 0.23 and 0.02. It is then easy to see that 0.02 is the smallest.	Ordering decimals, page 8
28	24	If $144 \div 3 = 48$ then $144 \div 6$ is half of 48 as you are dividing by a number twice as big.	
29	Triangle	You should imagine this happening to the cone: The remaining shape is a triangle.	
30	29	A prime number is a number that only has two factors – itself and 1. You do not find them in any multiplication tables except their own – and that for 1. Unfortunately there is no easy way to work them out. It is best to remember them. The first few are: 2, 3, 5, 7, 11, 13, 17, 19, 23, 29, 31, 37, 41, 43, 47, …	Properties of numbers, page 21

Mental arithmetic test A (Higher tiers)

Each question is worth 1 mark only.

Number	Answer	Tutorial	*Collins KS3 Maths Total Revision*
1	370	Multiplying numbers by 10 makes all the digits move one place to the left. Multiplying whole numbers by 10 is just like putting a zero on the end.	Multiplying and dividing by 10 and 100, page 5
2	0.25	You should know the equivalences between decimals, fractions and percentages.	Equivalent fractions, decimals and percentages, page 114
3	$\frac{6}{10}$ or any equivalent probability such as 60%, 0.6, $\frac{3}{5}$	This is about simple probability. 6 of the cubes are blue so there is a 6 out of 10 chance. You must write the answer in figures and not in words.	Simple probability, page 50
4	2500 m	You need to know your metric units and their relationships.	Metric units, page 87
5	49	You should know about BODMAS, which tells you to do the bracket first. The problem becomes 7×7. You also need to know your tables!	Tables, page 172 BODMAS, page 172
6	9.1	This is a simple addition of decimals. Normally you would line up the points but you probably won't have time to write the sum out, so a quick way is to add 3.6 to 5.4 which gives 9, then add on the 0.1 to get 9.1.	Decimals, page 8
7	48	25% is a quarter so the answer is $4 \times 12 = 48$.	Equivalent fractions and percentages, page 114
8	$2k + n$, or equivalent $(4k + 2n) \div 2$, $2k + 1n$ etc.	If $4k + 2n = 82$, then 41 is one-half of this, so $41 = (4k + 2n) \div 2$.	Basic algebra, page 75
9	$\frac{6}{10}$ or any equivalent fraction	Three-fifths ($\frac{3}{5}$) is equivalent to many fractions. You can find any of them by multiplying the top and bottom of the fraction by the same number. Multiplying by 2 gives $\frac{6}{10}$, multiplying by 10 gives $\frac{60}{100}$.	Fractions, page 64
10	30 cm^2	The area of a triangle is $\frac{1}{2} \times$ base $\times$ height. You need to know this formula.	Areas of shapes, page 147
11	$h = 21$	The calculation is $7 \times 6 \div 2$. It is easiest to do $6 \div 2 = 3$ first, then $7 \times 3 = 21$.	Substituting into simple formulae, page 24
12	1 or 0 or both	There are only two numbers which, if you square them, give the same number. These are 0 and 1.	
13	9	To solve the equation subtract 26 from both sides. This gives $^-2n = ^-18$, then divide by 2 to get $^-n = ^-9$, so $n = 9$.	Solving equations, page 124

Number	Answer	Tutorial	*Collins KS3 Maths Total Revision*
14	0.95	You should know that the probability of an event not happening is 1 minus the probability of that event happening. So P(not raining in August) = 1 – P(raining in August). 1 – 0.05 = 0.95	
15	4200	This is the calculation 60×70. The easy way to do this mentally is to multiply 6 by 7 (giving 42) and multiply by 100 (add two zeros at the end), to find the answer.	
16	$c = 13$	If the mean of three numbers is 10 then they must add up to 30. $6 + 11 = 17$ so the third number must be 13 as $30 - 17 = 13$.	Means (averages), page 93
17	$3y^2 + 18y$	This is called the distributive law. Each term in the bracket must be multiplied by the term outside the bracket. This gives $3y \times y + 3y \times 6$. You must work out the expressions.	Algebra, page 75
18	$100 \leqslant$ answer $\leqslant 105$	To make an estimate quickly you must round to give numbers that you can work with easily. In this case the problem is almost the same as $50 \div 0.5 = 500 \div 5 = 100$.	Estimating with decimals, page 167
19	523	You have to choose the largest value as the hundreds digit but because the answer has to be odd the 3 must be the last digit.	Place value, page 5
20	You should have circled 560 m	The median is the middle number when the numbers are arranged in order of size. You probably won't have time to write them out in order but here is a way of finding the median from a list. Cross off the largest and smallest, then cross off the next largest and smallest of the numbers that are left. Keep on doing this until eventually you will be left with one number (the median) or two numbers (the median is halfway between them). i.e. ~~820 m~~ 620 m ~~430 m~~ 560 m 550 m ~~820 m~~ ~~620 m~~ ~~430 m~~ 560 m ~~550 m~~	Medians and other averages, page 45
21	54.6	If $14 \times 39 = 546$ then 14×3.9 is 10 times smaller. Dividing 546 by 10 gives 54.6.	Multiplying and dividing by 10 and 100, page 5
22	162	You are not expected to know your 18 times table but you can do this two ways. Multiply 9×10 and 9×8 then add the answers. i.e. $90 + 72 = 162$, or work out 9×20 then subtract 9×2, i.e. $180 - 18 = 162$.	

Number	Answer	Tutorial	*Collins KS3 Maths Total Revision*
23	Circle, sphere, hemisphere or equivalent descriptions to circular.	Imagine the robot tied to a stake. The stake is at the centre of the circle and the length of the rope is the radius. The path traced by the free end of the rope is called the locus.	Loci, page 202
24	48°	You should know that the angles in a triangle add up to 180°. The calculation is $180 - (47 + 85) = 180 - 132 = 48$.	Angles, page 83
25	3 and 9	You should know that 'sum' means added together and 'product' means multiplied together. There are several pairs of numbers that add up to 9 (1 and 8, 2 and 7, 3 and 6, 4 and 5) but only one of these pairs multiplies together to give 27. You need to know your tables!	Tables, page 1
26	$21 \leq$ answer ≤ 23 m/s. e.g. 22 m/s	75 mph = 33 m/s so 25 mph = 11 m/s. $2 \times 25 = 50$ and $2 \times 11 = 22$	
27	You should have drawn an arrow pointing to this edge.	It is not easy to work out how a net fits together. If you haven't made all the nets of a cube you will probably find this difficult. You will not have time to make the net in the test but if you try it now you will see that the marked edge fits with edge A.	Nets and isometric projections, page 137
28	$\frac{1}{6}$	The calculation is $1 - (\frac{1}{2} + \frac{1}{3})$. You must know how to add fractions without a calculator. You need to be able to change the fractions so that they all have the same denominator (the bottom number). $\frac{1}{2} = \frac{3}{6}$ and $\frac{1}{3} = \frac{2}{6}$ so $\frac{3}{6} + \frac{2}{6} = \frac{5}{6}$ and $1 - \frac{5}{6} = \frac{1}{6}$.	
29	700	You are expected to know the 25 times table because it is an easy one. The key fact is that $4 \times 25 = 100$. $28 \div 4 = 7$, so $28 \times 25 = 700$.	
30	480 cm^3	If you double the lengths of a cuboid the volume increases by a factor of 8. (Each edge is twice as big and $2 \times 2 \times 2 = 8$.) You can do it like this if you know about volume scale factors (but this is level 8 work) or you can double the edges to $6 \times 8 \times 10$, then work it out. $6 \times 8 = 48$ so the answer is 480 cm^3.	Volumes of cuboids, page 147

Mental arithmetic test B (Higher tiers)

Each question is worth 1 mark only.

Number	Answer	Tutorial	Collins KS3 Maths Total Revision
1	7	You need to know your tables.	Multiplication tables, page 1
2	1000 ml	You need to know your metric units and their relationships.	Metric units and conversions, page 87
3	5	The calculation is 4×1.25. If you know that 0.25 is equivalent to a quarter it makes the problem much easier.	Equivalent fractions and decimals, page 114
4	$\frac{31}{36}$	You should know that the probability of an event not happening is 1 minus the probability of the event happening. So P(not getting a total of 8) = 1 – P(getting a total of 8).	Probability, page 161
5	£2.80	The easiest way to do this is by 'shopkeeper's addition'. Shopkeepers often used to count on until they got to the amount of money given, so £2.20 from £5 would be 80p make £3, and 2 more makes £5.	
6	You should have circled 3 feet.	You should know the conversion factors between metric units and imperial units. 1 metre is about 1 yard which is equal to 3 feet.	Metric and imperial units, page 87
7	10	The calculation is £3.70 ÷ 37p. It is probably easier to think of the problem as $10 \times 37p$ = £3.70.	Multiplying and dividing by 10 and 100, page 5
8	94°	You should know that there are 180° in the angle on a straight line. $180 - 86 = 94$.	Basic angles, page 83
9	84	If 35% of an amount is 42 then 70% is twice as much.	Percentages, page 64
10	$24\,cm^3$	The volume of a cuboid is length × width × height. The calculation in this case is $3 \times 2 \times 4 = 6 \times 4 = 24$.	Volumes of cuboids, page 147
11	8%	Per cent means 'out of 100'. 4 out of 50 is the same as 8 out of 100 so the answer is 8%.	Percentages, page 64
12	5100	Multiplying a decimal by 1000 causes all the digits to move three places to the left. You may think of it as moving the decimal point three places to the right. $5.1 \times 1000 = 5100$.	Multiplying and dividing by 10 and 100, page 5
13	8	You should imagine this picture.	

Number	Answer	Tutorial	Collins KS3 Maths Total Revision
14	3.42	The 'line' acts both as a division sign and a separator for the top and bottom. The bottom works out as 10. $34.2 \div 10 = 3.42$. Dividing a decimal by 10 causes all the digits to move one place to the right. You may think of it as moving the decimal point one place to the left.	
15	$b = ac$	This is cross-multiplication. The c on the bottom goes across and up to the top of the other side.	
16	7 499 999	You need to know that seven and a half million is 7 500 000. It is then a simple problem to work out.	Place value, page 5
17	Straight line, or straight or line	You need to imagine this picture. The path is called a locus.	Loci, page 202
18	15	If the probability of a train being late is 0.3 then this means that out of every 10 trains 3 will be late, or out of every 100 trains 30 will be late. Out of 50 trains 15 will be late. Another way of doing this is to multiply $50 \times 0.3 = 15$. This is the expected number of trains that will be late. Nothing is certain so if you said 'about 15' you would be right.	Probability, page 161
19	You should have these dots joined.	You just have to 'see' the square. Squares can sometimes be arranged like this. If you were looking for a square orientated like this ☐ you won't find one.	
20	$45 \leqslant$ answer $\leqslant 55$. e.g. 50	The sector of the pie chart for pupils who cycle is 25% or $\frac{1}{4}$. 25% of 200 is 50. You may be a little bit out if you think the sector is a bit over or under 25%.	Pie charts, page 96
21	640	You are not expected to know your 128 times table or to have enough time to work this out on paper. To do this sum do $5 \times 100 = 500$, then $5 \times 20 = 100$ then $5 \times 8 = 40$. These are added to give 640.	
22	31.2	If $234 \div 15 = 15.6$ then $468 \div 15$ is twice as big. $2 \times 15.6 = 31.2$.	

Number	Answer	Tutorial	*Collins KS3 Maths Total Revision*
23	$10 \leqslant$ answer $\leqslant 11$	To make an estimate quickly you must round to give numbers that you can work with easily. In this case the problem is almost the same as $500 \div 50 = 10$.	Estimating with decimals, page 167
24	4	You should realise that 2 tiles of side 50 cm fit down each side of the square metre. This means that $2 \times 2 = 4$ tiles are needed.	Area, page 36
25	5 or $^-5$	$d^2 = 2 \times 8 + 9 = 25$. $\sqrt{25} = 5$ or $^-5$.	Solving equations, page 124
26	$4t$	If the area is t^2 then the side is t. The perimeter is then $t + t + t + t = 4t$. This is a combination of algebra and areas of shapes.	Algebra, page 24 Areas, page 36
27	17	$2^3 + 3^2 = 8 + 9 = 17$. This is about powers. The calculation is $2 \times 2 \times 2 + 3 \times 3$.	
28	$10 \leqslant$ answer $\leqslant 13$	To make an estimate quickly you must round to give numbers that you can work with easily. In this case the problem is almost the same as $\dfrac{100 \times 0.5}{\sqrt{16}} = \dfrac{50}{4} \approx \dfrac{50}{5}$. You have to make the numbers easy enough so that you can do the estimate mentally.	Estimating with decimals, page 167
29	$t - 2$	$m + 7 = t$. If we do the same thing to both sides and take away 2 we get $m + 7 - 2 = t - 2$, so $m + 5 = t - 2$.	Solving equations, page 124
30	3.7 or equivalent	One number is a fraction. It is easier if you make this into a decimal. (3.4). If you think of the numbers on a number line you can see that 3.7 is halfway between them.	

Key Stage 3 Mathematics 1998
Mental Arithmetic Test C

First Name ....

Last Name ....

School ....

Pupil Number							Total Marks	

Time: 10 seconds

8	£		8

9		18 7 12	9

10		10

11		$21 - n = 8$	11

12			12

Time: 5 seconds

1		1

2		2

3	cm	3

4		4

5		5

6	$6y = 66$	6

7	732	7

13	%	Car Cycle Bus Walk	13

14		2cm ☐ 2cm 6cm ☐ 6cm	14

15	£	£52 £19	15

Time: 10 seconds

16	£	£3.49	16

17	hours	17

18		18

19	cm	30cm	19

20	years	1887 1920	20

21		30 ÷ (6 − 3)	21

22	4km 8km 12km 16km	22

23	£	£30	23

Time: 15 seconds

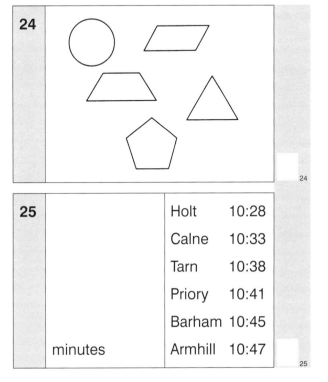

24		24

25		Holt 10:28 Calne 10:33 Tarn 10:38 Priory 10:41 Barham 10:45	
	minutes	Armhill 10:47	25

26	circle rectangle square rhombus triangle	26

27	0.2 0.1 0.28 0.23 0.02	27

28		144 ÷ 3 = 48	28

29		29

30		30

Key Stage 3 Mathematics 1998
Mental Arithmetic Test A

First Name ....

Last Name ....

School ....

Pupil Number [ ][ ][ ][ ][ ][ ]   Total Marks [ ]

Time: 10 seconds

5		$7 \times (3 + 4)$	5
6		5.4 3.7	6
7			7
8		$4k + 2n$ 82	8
9		$\dfrac{3}{5}$	9

Time: 5 seconds

1			1
2			2
3		4 red 6 blue	3
4	m		4

10		cm^2 10cm 6cm	10
11	$h =$	$h = \dfrac{7m}{2}$	11
12		$x^2 = x$	12
13		$26 - 2n = 8$	13
14		0.05	14
15		70	15

119

Time: 10 seconds

16	$c =$	10 $a = 6 \quad b = 11$	16
17		$3y(y + 6)$	17
18		$\dfrac{50.6}{0.49}$	18

Time: 15 seconds

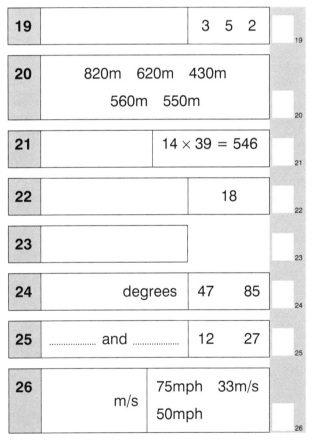

19		3 5 2	19
20	820m 620m 430m 560m 550m		20
21		$14 \times 39 = 546$	21
22		18	22
23			23
24	degrees	47 85	24
25	.... and	12 27	25
26	m/s	75mph 33m/s 50mph	26

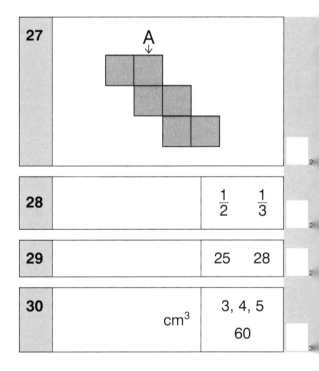

27	A ↓		
28		$\dfrac{1}{2}$ $\dfrac{1}{3}$	
29		25 28	
30	cm³	3, 4, 5 60	

Key Stage 3 Mathematics 1998
Mental Arithmetic Test B

First Name ....

Last Name ....

School ....

Pupil
Number [ ][ ][ ][ ][ ][ ]   Total
Marks [ ]

Time: 5 seconds

1		

2		ml

3		1.25

4		$\frac{5}{36}$

Time: 10 seconds

5	£

6	0.3 feet	3 feet	30 feet	300 feet

7		£3.70

8	degrees	

9		35% 42

10	cm³	4cm 3cm 2cm

11	%	4 50

12		5.1

13		

14		$\dfrac{34.2}{2.8 + 7.2}$

15	$b =$	$a = \dfrac{b}{c}$

Time: 10 seconds

16			16

17		17

18		0.3 50	18

Time: 15 seconds

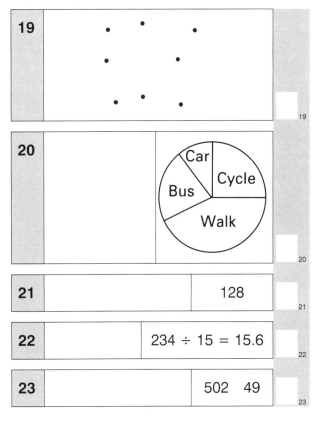

19	19

20	20

21	128	21

22	234 ÷ 15 = 15.6	22

23	502 49	23

24	50cm	2

25	$d =$	$d^2 = 2c + 9$	2

26	t^2	2

27	$x = 2, y = 3$ $x^y + y^x$	2

28	$\dfrac{103 \times 0.44}{\sqrt{16.1}}$	2

29	$m + 7 = t$	2

30	$3\frac{2}{5}$ 4	3